List of Contributors

Clive Archer is Research Professor, Department of Politics and Philosophy, Manchester Metropolitan University.

David Arter is Professor of Nordic Studies at the University of Aberdeen.

Francisco Granell is Director of Taskforce Enlargement at the European Commission, Brussels.

Lee Miles is Lecturer in Politics and Deputy Director of the Centre for European Union Studies (CEUS) at the University of Hull.

David Phinnemore is Lecturer in European Studies at Manchester Hope University College.

Christopher Preston is Project Director of the Know-How Fund, EU Integration Programme in Poland.

John Redmond is Reader in European Studies and Jean Monnet Chair in the Political Economy of European Integration at the University of Birmingham.

Adrian Treacher is a Research Associate with the Security Studies Research Programme at the University of Birmingham.

Preface

The principal issue faced by the European Union (EU) in the 1990s is how it can successfully combine deepening (accelerating European integration) and widening (embracing new members). As both processes intensify in the 1990s - deepening, because of the Maastricht Treaty and the 1996 intergovernmental conference, and widening, because of the growing numbers of countries wishing to join the EU - it becomes increasingly difficult to avoid addressing the issues that the EU has preferred to ignore with previous enlargements. The 1995 enlargement marks an important watershed for the EU. On the one hand, in practical terms, it is the last of the 'classical' or 'traditional' enlargements whereby new members are simply added on to the existing EU framework of institutions, policies and processes. On the other hand, in symbolic terms, it is the first of the new, post-Maastricht, enlargements which will make significant changes in the EU inevitable; it therefore marks the beginning of a crucial phase in the evolution of the EU.

However, at the same time, it also concludes an important stage in the evolution of EU-EFTA (European Free Trade Association) relations. This is a pivotal relationship in Europe, of great importance to both sides, and the 1995 accession of three EFTA members brings to an end a development which began in 1984 and which has brought the two sides closer together. A book on the 1995 enlargement and the build-up to it is therefore important as both a chronicle of a major period in EU-EFTA relations and, more generally, the history of Europe, and as an analysis of a crucial phase in the evolution of the EU.

Essentially, the book seeks to do three things:

(i)   Outline the evolution of EU-EFTA relations, particularly since 1984 (leading up to the European Economic Area), showing how four EFTA countries reached the stage of applying for EU membership;

(ii)   Analyze the four countries' negotiations to join the EU focusing on the process, issues and content, and the subsequent referenda;

(iii)   Set the 1995 enlargement in the wider context of the future widening (and deepening) of the EU.

The core of the book is simultaneously defined in both geographical and thematic terms.   Each of the contributors was assigned a country and also one or more issues that were particularly important for that country.

Much of the subject matter covered by this book is evolving as the EU evolves, and in some areas quite rapidly.   However, whilst it can never be possible to be completely up-to-date many of the issues and positions of participants change only slowly.   More importantly, the 1995 enlargement of the EU was an historical event in the development of the EU and the wider Europe.   If this book can have any lasting value it is as an account of this event - as a snapshot in time, cataloguing the issues, arguments, players and outcomes.

Most of the papers were given at a conference organised by the University Association for Contemporary European Studies at King's College, London in December 1994.   I am indebted to UACES and to the participants at that conference, and also to Edward Mortimer of the Financial Times who gave the closing address.   Finally, I would like to express my particular thanks to Adrian Treacher, my colleague at Birmingham, who, in addition to co-authoring the conclusion, also prepared camera ready copy of the book, proofread it and prepared the index.

1 Introduction

JOHN REDMOND

A brief history of enlargement

In the mid-1980s a significant enlargement of the European Union (EU) appeared to be an unlikely prospect. Virtually every potentially eligible European country that had not already joined was excluded by political constraint (membership of the Soviet bloc), by deliberate decision (membership of EFTA) or by their internal situation (Turkey, Malta and Cyprus). However, in the late 1980s the unthinkable began to happen and, over the subsequent few years, at least 18 aspiring members emerged, many of which have now submitted formal applications. These divide into three distinct groups:

- The EFTAns: Austria, Finland, Norway, Sweden and Switzerland all went on to make formal applications (although Norway ultimately decided not to join and the Swiss application is effectively suspended).
- The CEECs (central and eastern European countries), of which the frontrunners currently appear to be Poland, Hungary, the Czech Republic and Slovenia. The other recognised 'contenders' are Slovakia, Bulgaria, Romania, Latvia, Lithuania and Estonia. (However, this list may grow to include, for example, Croatia and Albania.)
- The Mediterranean applicants - Turkey, Malta and Cyprus - whose applications actually pre-date those of everyone else (except Austria).

Obviously, these membership bids were partly driven by a number of country and group-specific reasons but by themselves these would have been insufficient. The primary force was the impact of two radical changes within Europe. The most historic of these was clearly the momentous changes in central and eastern Europe - the end of the Cold War, the collapse of the Soviet bloc (and Union) and, effectively, the reunification of Europe. This opened possibilities that had been blocked for some of the EFTAns and for all the CEECs. Europe became a very different place.

The second change was internal to the EU: there was a resurgence of European integration. This began with the Single European Act and the Single European Market (SEM) programme and has culminated (so far) in the (Maastricht) Treaty of European Union (TEU). The SEM, in particular, concentrated minds. It was not merely the fear of 'Fortress Europe' and a consequent exclusion from EU markets but also a desire to benefit from the SEM's wider benefits. Virtually every country in the world felt the need to reassess its relationship with the EU and, for those in Europe, full membership of the EU was increasingly perceived as the best option. More fundamentally, this resurgence established beyond doubt the superiority of the EU over alternative forms of cooperation within Europe. The EU moved from being the major to the only significant player in Europe and Europe's voice in the wider world. This was abundantly clear in the GATT Uruguay Round which was essentially a debate between the EU and the USA.

In fact, EU enlargement has been a progressive and virtually continuous process. The first formal applications were submitted in 1961, only three years after the European Economic Community was established. Since that date, there have been few points in time when the EU was not either considering, negotiating terms with, or absorbing one or more new members. There have been three 'waves':

(i)   The first 'northern' group - Britain, Denmark and Ireland joined in 1973.
(ii)   A Mediterranean group joined in the 1980s - Greece in 1981 and Spain and Portugal in 1986.
(iii)   The second 'northern' wave - Austria, Finland and Sweden - which joined in 1995 and whose accession is the subject of this book.

Of course, Norway negotiated accession in both 1973 and 1995 but elected not to join on each occasion, after the terms of membership had been rejected in a popular referendum.

There are clearly similarities between the new members of 1973 and 1995. On the 'positive' side, Ireland can be portrayed as a good example of how a small, neutral country can participate enthusiastically in European integration, thereby diversifying its markets and reaping considerable advantage. On the 'negative' side, Britain and Denmark are examples of countries which are interested in European integration from a primarily economic perspective, with little interest in political integration because of a preference for intergovernmentalism and a reluctance to give up national sovereignty. Thus, history suggests that the 1995 enlargement may push the EU towards more integration in some (particularly economic) areas but within a more intergovernmental framework or, at the very least, against a backdrop of slower political integration.

However, it is dangerous to draw too many parallels because the European Union of 1995 and the world within which it operates are so radically different to the European Community of 1973 and its surrounding environment. The 1995 enlargement requires a more specific examination. In particular, this EFTAn group was quite different in a key respect to the other two groups of aspiring EU members which emerged in the late 1980s and early 1990s. Unlike the CEEC and Mediterranean applicants which essentially chose to apply for EU membership as soon as political and economic constraints were relaxed sufficiently to make membership a possibility, the EFTAns changed their minds. They had implicitly chosen not to join the fledgling EU in the late 1950s by creating EFTA and, indeed, the Norwegians had explicitly chosen not to join in their 1972 referendum.

The return of the prodigal sons: EFTA changes its mind

Whilst the volte-face of the EFTAns was quite remarkable, the attitude of the EU was no less striking. The EU welcomed rapprochement with EFTA with open arms (even though it did not initially offer full membership). Moreover, it quickly became clear that members of EFTA headed the EU's preferred pecking order as they were allowed to overtake the Mediterranean applicants[1] and joined the EU before the problems of absorbing the CEECs began to be addressed.

The reasons for this were obvious: the EFTAns share(d) a number of characteristics which made their accession to the EU highly appropriate, easily attainable and probably desirable:

- EFTA had a unique trading relationship with the EU in that not only was the EU its principal trading partner (which remains true of most European and, indeed, some non-European states), but EFTA was also the EU's major trading partner, accounting for as much EU trade as the USA and Japan combined. Thus it was mutually advantageous for members of both groups to facilitate reciprocal access to each others' markets.

- EFTA was comprised of rich, developed and democratic nations of a similar size to some existing EU member states.
- The EFTAns were all sufficiently rich to be net contributors to the EU budget. This is obviously not a necessary condition for successful accession to the EU but it is very helpful.
- Many of the EFTA countries were already well integrated economically into the EU, arguably more so than some of the EU's peripheral members, such as Greece.
- More fundamentally, for much of its existence, the EU has been a club for western European democracies and the absence of the EFTA states was considered an anomaly.

On the other hand, there were other shared characteristics which were potentially problematical:

- The shift to favouring EU accession was led by Governments; this backfired in the cases of Norway and (spectacularly) Switzerland as their general populations adopted the opposite point of view. More generally, even in those EFTAns which did eventually become EU members, there was sufficient scepticism to suggest difficulties (along British and Danish lines) in the future.
- Members of EFTA actually subsidised their agricultural sectors more than the EU. This ran counter to current trends to reduce farming subsidies within the EU because of pressures originating both internally (the excessive cost of the Common Agricultural Policy [CAP]) and externally (the Uruguay Round trade negotiations).
- Finally, as already indicated, the decision to pursue EU membership represented a complete reversal of policy. Until very recently, they had all rejected this course of action either implicitly by choosing to join EFTA or explicitly by voting not to join the EU in a referendum (in the case of Norway) or even the European Economic Area (EEA) (in the case of Switzerland).

This last point is potentially of great consequence because it raises questions about the reasons why the EFTAns chose to pursue EU accession in the 1990s. These countries approach EU membership with a degree of ambivalence and this has been characterised by Kelstrup's 'integration dilemma' argument.[2] The 'integration dilemma' assumes that a state is confronted with the choice of either giving up substantial parts of its sovereignty with the danger of being 'entrapped' within European integration or insisting on its independence with the danger of being 'abandoned' and isolated from the integration process.[3] The suggestion is thus that the EFTAns chose EU membership not because of positive feelings about European integration but for the negative reason that, whilst not sharing the ideals of the EU's founding fathers, they nevertheless wished to join the EU because they wished to avoid the costs of non-membership. This has important implications for the future development of the EU (which are taken up in the conclusion).

This is, to some extent, illustrated by the reasons why the EFTA countries decided to apply to join the EU.[4] The initial driving force was the single market or more specifically fear of exclusion from it. It was not just a question of concern about restrictions to market access but also the consequent loss of economies of scale and attractiveness to foreign investors and, furthermore, the exclusion from the EU's public procurement market. A second important catalyst was the collapse of the Soviet bloc which had both an important political impact - it relaxed the neutrality constraint for the EFTA neutrals - and significant economic ramifications - some EFTA countries were faced with a need to strengthen economic links with the West to replace their trade with eastern Europe. Allied to these fundamental economic and political forces was a growing sense that the EU was 'Europe' and a related 'bandwagon' effect as the application of one country seemed inevitably to trigger that of its neighbour(s).

However, two members of EFTA remained aloof from the general euphoria - Iceland and Switzerland, although the latter did briefly flirt with membership - and it is perhaps worth dwelling briefly on these two (as they are not covered by the main body of the book). The seventh EFTA member - Liechtenstein - has not ruled out a membership bid in the future and clearly wants to strengthen its ties with the EU. Its participation in the EEA went ahead in spite of the awkward ramifications for its relationship with Switzerland caused by the latter's rejection of the EEA. In fact, the accession of Liechtenstein to the EU in 1995 was almost certainly precluded by its size; the admission of any micro-state to the EU must await the necessary institutional reforms which have to be agreed by the existing membership.

Iceland could also have faced problems with its size although this never actually arose as it did not seriously consider applying for membership.[5] The main reason for this stemmed from the country's economic dependence on fish. Accession would have implied participation in the EU's Common Fisheries Policy and accepting the principle of open access to Icelandic fishing waters for all EU fishermen. This was judged too high a price to pay for the benefits of EU membership. A parallel can be drawn with the case of Greenland which, shortly after receiving internal autonomy (from Denmark) in 1979, chose to leave the EU for similar reasons.[6]

Of course, there were also other considerations. Iceland has traditionally remained outside the mainstream of international politics and has reflected its geographical position by maintaining links with both Europe and the United States, on which it relies for its security (through membership of the North Atlantic treaty Organisation. Moreover, Iceland only became fully independent in 1944 and guards its sovereignty jealously, which it fears could be heavily constrained by membership of the EU - '[t]hey could buy Iceland in an afternoon',[7] the Icelandic Prime Minister has said. Any lingering doubts that the Icelandic position may change in the immediate future were removed when the Norwegians rejected accession to the EU in a referendum. This removed the one prospect that might have driven the Icelanders into the arms of the EU (that their main competitor would join the EU and receive open access to the EU's market for fish).

The Swiss case is completely different but no less clear-cut. Switzerland, has always had some difficulties with the EU because of disputes over the transit of EU lorries and the associated environmental problems. More fundamentally, there are five critical barriers that would have to be overcome before Swiss accession to the EU would be possible:[8]

- neutrality - this is particularly important in Switzerland;
- federalism: considerable powers are devolved to the cantons which would create institutional problems but, without which, it is feared that Switzerland would disintegrate into its French, German and Italian speaking components;
- policies towards foreigners: the Swiss fear being swamped by foreign nationals and, in particular, the selling off of land to foreigners;
- agriculture: in common with other EFTA countries Switzerland subsidises agriculture much more than the EU does;
- direct democracy: this is highly valued in Switzerland, particularly the use of referenda, but could probably not survive EU membership.

The difficulties are so great that the Swiss could not even join the EEA; a majority voted against membership in a referendum in December 1992.

Thus both Iceland and Switzerland are arguably 'special cases' which are likely to continue to distance themselves from the European mainstream in the immediate future for their own particular reasons. Instead they seem satisfied with relationships with the EU which fall short of full membership - the EEA for Iceland and a 'third way' for Switzerland. However, in the case of other EFTAns and, indeed, many aspiring EU members, it is actually the perception that there are no viable alternatives to full EU membership which has finally pushed them to apply to join.

Alternatives to EU membership

European states eligible for EU membership have basically a choice of five possible kinds of relationship with the EU which are (in ascending order of the degree of integration with the EU):

(i)   a trade agreement;
(ii)   a 'third way';
(iii)   association;
(iv)   membership of the EEA;
(v)   full membership.

The first of these - a trade agreement - is a very rudimentary and simple arrangement and is increasingly being used as an initial stepping stone for the CEECs on their way to a much deeper relationship with the EU. It is no longer seen as a final form of linkage with the EU. The 'third way' is a form of extendable trade agreement which has been pioneered by (and is possibly unique to) Switzerland. No other country appears to favour this kind of link - quite probably because they lack the wealth and importance (to the EU) of Switzerland - although the Maltese Labour Party favours a kind of special relationship for Malta, short of full membership, which seems to fall into this middle ground and the Swedes expressed an interest in something of this nature in the late 1960s. In a sense, the 'third way' approximates to association for the rich, independent and 'strong', but has to be called something different as association tends to be for the poor, dependent and 'weak'.

However, association has been sought by EFTA members in the past - for example by Austria and Sweden in the 1960s - and several EFTAns have been associate members of the various EU exchange rate mechanisms. Unfortunately, there are two immediate difficulties with association. First, it is generally not considered as an end in itself but rather as a holding mechanism for countries not yet ready to join the EU, but with full membership as their ultimate objective; this was quite explicitly the case with the first two agreements with Greece and Turkey and also in the recent European Agreements with the CEECs. To that extent, association was never likely to appeal to EFTA members in the past when they did not want to join and remained unattractive for those who changed their minds and applied to join the EU in the 1990s (since they did not wish to wait). In fact, when French President de Gaulle suggested association as an alternative to membership for Britain - then a member of EFTA - in the 1960s, it was taken as a kind of insult. Second, association agreements have all failed in the past. Clearly, they were doomed by the military interventions in Turkey, Greece and Cyprus and by the election of a strongly anti-EU government in Malta shortly after the association agreement was signed. However, in the one case where the agreement ran for some years unimpeded by such specific problems - Turkey - there was also clear evidence of procrastination on the EU side.[9]   Thus no association agreement has ever run its full course and achieved the free trade area or customs union for which it was designed. Indeed, to some extent, this is not surprising since, other than as a vehicle for full membership, association is arguably a dubious privilege. It is nowhere formally defined[10] but, in practice, appears to consist of:

- The phased establishment of a free trade area or a customs union;
- Limited EU financial assistance;
- Harmonisation or alignment of economic and related policies;
- Association institutions at Council and Parliament level;
- Political dialogue;
- Cultural dialogue.

What is noticeably lacking is any access to significant amounts of EU financial assistance - notably the structural funds - and any voice in the EU's decision-making processes. Thus association could amount to much of the pain of integration with the EU - particularly through giving market access to competitors from the EU - with little of the gain; whether it is structural fund monies or exclusion from EU decision-making that matters the most will vary, with the EFTAns being more concerned with the latter (and the CEECs and the Mediterranean applicants with the former). Moreover, associate agreements are subject to various exclusions - and the

EU has been quite prepared to invoke them - ; which further emphasises the less than full rights enjoyed by associate members.

In principle, the EEA is a much more equitable relationship but, in practice, it still falls well short of true equality and is similarly incomplete in a number of key respects. It was actually created as a genuine alternative to membership. For the EFTAns, it would allow full participation in the EU's single market by an extension of the four freedoms of movement (goods, services, people and capital), involvement in the so-called 'flanking' policies[11] and a more formal institutional framework through the EEA institutions. The EU, on the other hand, was enabled to continue its renewed forward momentum and focus on deepening (through the Maastricht agenda), without the distraction of having to accommodate new members; there was also a beneficial side-effect in the shape of the financial mechanism by which the (richer) EFTAns were to compensate the poorer EU members for access to their markets. Unfortunately, the EEA proved as difficult to negotiate as EU membership and the dominance of the EU was reflected in both the negotiations and their outcome. EFTAn demands for derogations, specific safeguard clauses and measures to preserve their higher standards in the fields of the environment, consumer protection, and health and safety were virtually ignored. Even more fundamentally, the EFTA countries were given no role in the determination of the rules of the EEA which are simply extensions of EU rules, laid down by full EU members; thus the EFTA side of the EEA is not directly involved in decision-making. In a sense, the EFTAns could lose more sovereignty by participating in the EEA than they would by becoming full members of the EU.

From an EFTAn perspective, the EEA is thus a fundamentally flawed concept. This is also true of association, the 'third way' and trade agreements. These are all very unequal relationships with the balance very much fixed in favour of the EU. The terms of the agreements and the concessions offered are mainly determined by the EU, and are hedged by safeguard and escape clauses which the EU is not slow to use. Ultimately, the key point is that over the last 50 years Europe has evolved in such a way that the EU has become by far the most powerful force within it. Non-members are therefore faced with a choice: they can accept their subservience and opt for a lesser relationship, but most sovereign states are loathe to do this unless they are small or feel able to stand apart from the EU (such as Switzerland and, eventually, Norway); consequently, they pursue membership although possibly for the wrong reasons (the 'integration dilemma'). Alternatively, and more commonly, they opt for membership as their preferred option in the first place, in which case anything short of accession is unsatisfactory even on a temporary basis. Any relationship short of full membership of the EU thus becomes an inferior option, except in a few very particular cases. By the 1990s this certainly appeared to be true for Austria, Finland, Norway and Sweden.

Plan of the book

The book consists of two groups of chapters. The four middle chapters deal with the four applicant countries individually while also seeking to cover one or more specific issues relevant to all four countries, but which is or are especially pertinent for the country being covered by that particular chapter. The other group comprises the present chapter, the next two and the conclusion, and deals with general issues which are relevant to all countries joining the EU. Thus, in chapter 2, Preston catalogues the evolution of relations between the EU and EFTA, which he divides into three phases: 1960-84, 1984-89 and 1989-94. He charts the gradual rapprochement of the EU and EFTA, through the Luxembourg process, the Interlaken principles and the EEA, to the point when accession to the EU seemed the only viable option to much of the EFTAn membership. In chapter 3, Granell, who was actually involved in the accession negotiations (on the EU side), takes up the story. He begins by setting the 1995 enlargement in the broader historical context of past enlargements of the EU and then, after a brief survey of the EEA, provides a detailed account and analysis of the process and content of the enlargement negotiations with the four applicant countries.

The four country chapters (4-7) follow the same basic pattern:

- an examination of the country's particular motivations and problems;
- a description and analysis of the country's referendum;
- an analysis of the difficulties raised by the issue(s) attached to the chapter, for the country, and also for the other three.

Chapter 4 deals with Austria, transit and the environment. Austria was the first of the EFTAns to apply to join the EU (in 1989) and, from the onset, tended to view the EEA mainly as a stepping stone to full EU membership. Nevertheless, the referendum campaign was difficult for those who supported accession, although the Austrians eventually voted in favour by a substantial margin. All this is reported by Phinnemore who also describes the rather complex compromise on transit - an issue of concern exclusively to Austria - and highlights the centrality of environmental concerns to all three new members.

In chapter 5, Miles considers Sweden and security issues. He begins by examining the concept of neutrality and what it means for each of the three new members; he then provides a brief history of Sweden's relations with the EU and analyses the Swedish referendum; finally, he returns to security and considers the implications of the 1995 enlargement for the EU's Common Foreign and Security Policy. In chapter 6, Arter charts the radical shifts in Finnish fortunes and policies which culminated in Finland's application for EU membership and then analyses the referendum in Finland and the debate surrounding it. The final part of the chapter focuses on agriculture. In the last of the 'country chapters' (7), Archer considers the unique case of Norway where history repeated itself as the population voted once again not to join the EU. The referendum is examined in detail and the chapter pays attention to two issues in particular - fisheries and energy.

Finally, the concluding chapter describes the changes to the EU's institutions made in 1995 to accommodate the three new members. It asserts that this kind of mechanical accession - the so-called 'classical' method of enlargement - is now a thing of the past, and future enlargements will be 'adaptive'. They will involve major changes in the EU's institutions and policies. The final sections consider some possible future scenarios and analyses the impact on and contribution of the three new members.

Notes

1.   Turkey (1987) applied before any EFTAns or CEECs and only Austria (1989) applied before Cyprus (1990) and Malta (1990).

2.   M. Kelstrup (1993) 'Small States and European Political Integration', in T. Tiilikainen and I. Petersen (eds) *The Nordic Countries and the European Community*, pp. 136-62. Copenhagen: Copenhagen Political Studies Press.

3.   This argument has been developed in the context of enlargement in L. Miles, J. Redmond and R. Schwok 'Integration Theory and the Enlargement of the European Union' in S. Mazey and C. Rhodes, eds, *The State of the European Community* (American) European Community Studies Association's third biannual volume, Lynne Rienner, 1995, and L. Miles and J. Redmond 'Enlarging the European Union: The Erosion of Federalism?' *Cooperation and Conflict* September, 1996.

4.   The rationale for individual countries is taken up in detail in the subsequent chapters.

5.   In fact, had it done so, the EU would have faced something of a dilemma. Whilst, on the one hand, Iceland is a micro-state - comparable, in terms of population, with Malta, for example - on the other hand, had Iceland applied with Sweden, Finland and Norway, it is difficult to see how the Icelanders could have been rejected.

6.   For details, see F. Nicholson and R. East (1987) *From the Six to the Twelve: the enlargement of the European Communities* (Longman: Harlow, Essex), pp. 207-11.

7.   Maria Romantschuk (1990) 'Island är inte till salu (Iceland Not For Sale)', *Hufvudstadsbladet*, 6 October.

8.   For more detail, see R. Schwok (1991) *Switzerland and the European Common Market* (New York: Praeger), pp. 107-15.

9.   See J. Redmond (1993) The Next Mediterranean Enlargement of the European Community (Dartmouth: Aldershot), pp. 23-31.

10.   Article 238 of the Treaty of Rome (EEC) is rather vague. It refers to 'creating ... reciprocal rights and obligations, joint actions and special procedures' but does not specify in any detail what form these should take.

11.   The fields of joint action are research and technological development, information services, the environment, education, training and youth, social policy, consumer protection, small and medium-sized enterprises, tourism, the audio-visual sector and civil protection. See Council and Commission of the EC's (1992) *Agreement on the European Economic Area*, Luxembourg: Office for Official Publications of the ECs, Article 78.

2 EFTA, the EU and the EEA

CHRISTOPHER PRESTON

Introduction

The applications for full EU membership made by Austria, Norway, Sweden and Finland, between 1989 and 1992 mark the end of an historic division of western Europe into two trading blocs. Whilst Switzerland and Iceland chose not to apply for EU membership, the four applications in effect resolved the tension that had existed between the EU and EFTA for over thirty years in favour of the former. As the major source of new EU members over that period, the fourth enlargement provided conclusive proof that the EU model of integration has proved more robust, and ultimately better able to meet the long-term needs of European states than the looser EFTA model.

Yet in order to understand why these four states applied for EU membership it is important to examine the development of EU/EFTA relations over this period, to look at the various attempts to reconcile two differing models of economic and political cooperation, and to understand the wider contextual factors which led to the erosion of EFTA. Three key themes underpin this paper:

- From its inception EFTA was always seen by its members as a pragmatic alternative to full EU membership. Despite its achievements, its outlook was essentially reactive, concentrating on managing the spillover effects of EU integration, rather than putting forward a radical alternative model of economic and political development.
- Membership of EFTA was shaped more by political factors, in particular its members' attitudes to sovereignty, and in some cases neutrality, than by any compelling economic logic. As the broader geopolitical picture in Europe evolved, so economic self interest shifted the balance, albeit at different speeds in different members in favour of EU membership.

- Attempts to integrate the two groups, and blur their organisational boundaries, most particularly through the European Economic Area (EEA) Agreement only highlighted the imbalance between the EU and EFTA, and further undermined the long-term credibility of EFTA.

Three phases to EU/EFTA relations can be identified:

1960 - 1984: This first phase lasted from the formation of EFTA, at the Stockholm Convention of 1960 to the start of the "Luxembourg process" in 1984, in which EFTA sought a more broadly based multilateral dialogue with the EU, beyond the tariff and quota removals between the two groups which had hitherto been the basis of their bilateral relations. During that period both groups had given priority to their own, internal integration policies. Agreements between them were focused on avoiding excessive trade diversion and dealing with the spillover consequences of the EU's first and second enlargement. During this period the two trade blocs largely coexisted comfortably. Despite the net loss of EFTA members to the EU neither group represented a fundamental threat to the other's existence.

1984 - 1989: This second phase lasted from the start of the Luxembourg process until Jacques Delors' proposal in 1989 to create a European Economic Area encompassing the two groups. Despite the intensification of relations between the EU and EFTA within the Luxembourg process, the piece meal approach failed to keep up with the pace of events. The EU's proposals for a Single European Market (SEM), published in 1985, together with the commitment to further deepening, implicit in the Single European Act (SEA) of 1987, and the Iberian enlargement of 1984 marked a new phase of dynamism in the Community's development. This presented EFTA members with a series of acute dilemmas, since they wished to participate in the economic processes of the SEM but without becoming full EU members.

1989 - 1994: This third phase lasted from the initial EEA proposal up to the implementation of the Agreement, by which time full accession negotiations with the four EFTA applicants were themselves almost complete. This period was characterised by the exhaustive, and ultimately fruitless attempts to reconcile EFTA members' preference for participation in the integration process without the constraints of full membership. From the EU's perspective it represented an attempt to sustain the momentum of deepening at a time when external pressures, both from EFTA, and from eastern Europe became more pressing. By 1992 the logic of further enlargement became overwhelming, with full accession negotiations opening in 1993.

In retrospect the process whereby the EU came to absorb EFTA might seem almost inevitable, given the power imbalance between them, which became more visible as the EU enlarged in the 1970s and 1980s. Yet, although many of the contextual, particularly economic, trends were evident at the time it can be argued that full accession only became a serious option after 1991 once the inadequacies of the EEA proposal became clearer, and once public opinion in the EFTA states accepted that national interests were better served as full EU members than in the outer ring of an emerging model of concentric circles.

1960 - 1984: The origins of EFTA and the response to European Integration

The origin of the division of western Europe into two trade blocs lies in the debates of the 1950s about the most appropriate model for ensuring pan-European political stability and economic prosperity. Two schools of thought were evident at the time. The integrationists, led by France and strongly supported by the Germans, exemplified by the views of Jean Monnet and Robert Schumann, favoured a strong political union, based on a customs union with internal Community trade preference. Sectoral integration, starting with coal, steel and agriculture, but moving to other sectors would ensure the momentum of the project. The multilateralists, led by the UK, strongly supported by the Nordic Countries and the Swiss wanted a looser free trade area which would neither constrain their own external trade policies, nor compromise their political independence.

British underestimation of the strength of the integrationists' commitment to a strong political union has been well documented.[1] The UK only sent a representative, with observer status to the critical Messina Conference of 1955, rather than a delegate with a decision-making mandate. Following the ratification of the Treaty of Rome in 1957 the OEEC, strongly encouraged by the British, set up a committee to explore the feasibility of a wider European free trade area encompassing the inner six Rome Treaty signatories and those countries which did not share their integrationist ambitions.

Negotiations, known as the Maudling talks continued from 1957 to 1959 and discussed numerous models for reconciling the inner EC customs union with the outer free trade area. However despite careful consideration, no realistic framework could be found which combined the aim of external tariff harmonisation, integral to the customs union model, with the preservation of external tariff autonomy implicit in the free trade area model.

In many respects these debates rehearsed those of the late 1980s in relation to the SEM and the EEA.[2] The inner core group were determined to press ahead with an ambitious economic and political project, and were unwilling to compromise their objectives for the sake of more diffuse European interests. The failure of the Maudling talks led the seven non-EC states, (Austria, the UK, Denmark, Norway, Portugal, Sweden, and Switzerland) to establish their own grouping, and in 1960 EFTA was formed.

The objectives of EFTA were always intended to be more limited than those of the EC, and were essentially to increase the bargaining weight of its members in their negotiations with the EC.[3] The reappraisal of British interests which, following the Macmillan government's view that De Gaulle's attitude would dilute the EC's supranationality, led to the UK's application for membership, was seen by the other EFTA members as a lack of commitment to the organisation's future. Given their trade dependency on the UK, Norway, Denmark and Ireland also applied for membership at the same time. Despite the rejection of the UK's applications in 1963 and 1967 the three continued to link their own applications to the UK's.

Despite EFTA's vulnerability to defections during the 1960s and 1970s it served its members' interests well enough. The accession of the UK Ireland and Denmark to the EU in 1973 led EFTA to negotiate a bilateral free trade agreement with the EU. The UK had made the maintenance of an open trading regime with its former EFTA partners a major priority of its accession negotiations and did not want trade diverting barriers re-erected.

Although the loss of the UK reduced EFTA's political weight, it still provided a vehicle for its remaining members' interests since its intergovernmental character allowed its members' diverse economic and geopolitical interests to be accommodated. Within the broader framework created by the 1973 FTAs (Free Trade Agreements), significant trade creation occurred, with inter bloc trade increasing faster than intra-bloc trade[4] without compromising EFTA members' concerns about supranationality.

1984-1989 New realities; A new dynamic Community and the Single European Market

By the early 1980s EFTA was confronted with a new set of dilemmas. The tariff and quantitative restrictions identified in the 1973 FTAs had been largely removed and EFTA was therefore searching for a new organisational role. The second enlargement negotiations with Greece had highlighted the need to negotiate better transit agreements with Austria.[5] The third enlargement negotiations with Spain and Portugal, though deadlocked over agricultural policy raised the prospect of a larger EU with a centre of political and economic gravity further to the south.

In 1984 EFTA proposed to the EU a new multilateral dialogue. Following a meeting in April both sides committed themselves to the development of the 'Luxembourg process', with the joint declaration setting out the intention to cooperate on the harmonisation of standards, the removal of technical barriers, the simplification of border formalities and to improved action against unfair competition. It also sought to go beyond trade issues and establish cooperation in research and development, working conditions, culture and the environment. A High Level Steering Group (HLSG) was established to demonstrate political commitment to the process.

The Luxembourg process achieved a number of practical objectives, including improved rules of origin, a Single Administrative Document for goods in transit and EFTA participation in Community R&D programmes. Yet the limitations of the Luxembourg process became much clearer after the publication of the Commission's White Paper on the Internal Market in 1985, and the serious negotiations on its implementation got underway in 1987-88.

The commitment of the EU to create a market free of internal barriers presented all the EU's major trading partners with a series of difficult challenges. The White Paper identified numerous non-tariff barriers to trade within the EU, including divergent technical standards, incompatible fiscal regimes and preferential and discriminatory public procurement policies. During the late 1980s it was unclear, at least to outsiders, how far the EU's internal liberalisation process might be accompanied by some degree of external protection. Whilst the fear of 'fortress Europe' was expressed most vociferously in the US, it was also acutely felt in EFTA countries. By the late 1980s the EU and EFTA had developed a pattern of symmetrical trade dependency with each group being the other's largest trading partner. Wijkman notes that it is impossible to identify which group a country belongs to solely on the basis of its trade patterns.[6] The Single Market proposals therefore raised genuine fears in EFTA that their terms of trade might deteriorate after 1992.

Whilst it was never likely that the trade gains in industrial goods following the 1973 FTAs would be wholly lost, concern focused on how far EFTA based companies would be able to participate in the dynamic gains, forecast by the Cecchini Report to flow from the industry restructuring that would follow the removal of artificial supply side barriers.   The emphasis given in the report's methodology to the importance of scale economies as a key determinant of competitive advantage was of particular concern to EFTA countries, given their comparatively small number of companies of global scale. In industries where they had such scale, for instance Swedish automobiles, or Swiss pharmaceuticals and financial services, economic self interest dictated that they should participate in this pan-European industry restructuring by whatever means.

These concerns led EFTA based companies to make substantial investments within the EU during this period. EFTA's outward Foreign Direct Investment (FDI) flows totalled 8 per cent of all the OECD's outward investment flows in the 1980s, making them the OECD's most active investors abroad, measured in relation to GDP per head.[7] During this period EFTA countries became net exporters of capital. In Sweden and Finland in particular investments abroad were, in the 1980s four times higher than investments received from abroad. Sweden and Switzerland were the major EFTA investors with four-fifths of EFTA's outward FDI stock being owned by them. Companies were motivated both by the fear that they might be explicitly excluded from the EU's internal market, and by the desire, most keenly felt in the Nordic countries, to be physically closer to the new market opportunities, most likely to arise in the core economies of the EU.

Despite the propensity of EFTA-based corporations to take their own initiatives, the internal market plan still presented EFTA as an organisation with a dilemma. At one of the HLSG meetings at Interlaken in 1987, the Commission set out three principles which, it said, should in future govern EU/EFTA relations. These were that priority should be given to the EU's own integration agenda, that the EU's decision-making autonomy must be preserved, and that a satisfactory balance of advantages and obligations should be maintained in each case. These 'Interlaken Principles' forced EFTA countries to consider the full political implications of their desire to participate in the internal market process. Wijkman identifies the 'dilemma of the favourite sons', in which '....the EFTA countries are present in the EU as invisible members'. In 1990 he argued that:

> The EFTA countries are bound to the Community by common economic concerns but have a different institutional preference. This institutional difference is more important than the disparate size of the organisations. EC/EFTA relations are characterised by asymmetric institutional powers in what is basically a complementary economic relationship. This poses a dilemma for the EFTA countries. Is institutional harmonisation the price for deepened integration with the EC?[8]

The domestic debate in EFTA countries

The late 1980s also saw a developing domestic debate in the EFTA countries about how far EU developments, and changes in the wider geopolitical environment demanded a fundamental reappraisal of their political and economic interests.

Norway

In Norway the debate was largely shaped by the traumatic experience of the 1972 referendum on EU membership. Official Norwegian policy was therefore very cautious. The government's European Report of May 1987 stated the intention to adapt to the development of the internal market 'as far as possible'. Developing the argument in Parliament in 1988, the Prime Minister Mrs Bruntlund stated that '...it is important that Norwegian society should be ready and able to discuss these challenges without being eclipsed by a new and premature debate on Norwegian membership of the Community'.[9] Whilst Norway's NATO membership meant that, from the EU's perspective there would have been no political constraints on closer integration, the Norwegians had a strong preference for pursuing a multilateral EFTA focused strategy towards the internal market.

Sweden

Swedish policy towards the EU was set out in the policy paper presented to the Swedish Parliament in 1987. It identified the economic impact of the internal market on Sweden and argued that unilateral alignment with EU rules might be necessary. However, given the lack of Parliamentary consensus on EU membership, the debate's conclusion, endorsed by the Foreign Affairs Committee was that ' ... membership of the Community is not an objective for the negotiations which are now starting ... ', the possibility of EU membership however was not excluded so long as it did not compromise the credibility of Sweden's neutrality policy.

Finland

Finnish policy towards the EU before 1989 was based on the need to reconcile its need to pursue closer economic ties with the EU without compromising its strategic relationship with the USSR, as defined in the 1948 Treaty of Friendship, Cooperation and Mutual Assistance. Whilst its trade links with the USSR helped to cushion its economy more than in Sweden's case, the economic rationale for closer engagement in the internal market was similar. The Finns were therefore strongly in favour of the Luxembourg process, with the government's November 1988 White Paper categorically rejecting EU membership as incompatible with neutrality.

Iceland

Icelandic policy towards the EU was largely determined by sovereignty and economic issues, particularly its dependence on fish exports which in the post-war period have constituted 70 to 90 per cent of the total value of its exports. Exchanging access to the internal market in return for EU access to fish resources, implicit in EU membership, had little attraction for Iceland, whilst the development of the EU's Common Fisheries Policy only hardened attitudes during the 1980s. Successive governments therefore ruled out EC membership.

Austria

Austrian policy towards the EU was shaped by its policy of permanent neutrality, enshrined in the 1955 State Treaty. However, by the late 1980s the economic arguments in favour of closer integration with the EU became more pressing, given Austria's central position, its close economic ties with Germany and its very high trade dependence on the EU. The Austrians openly considered the possibility of EU membership before the other EFTA members because of their conviction that only full participation in EU decision-making would secure their economic interests. In 1988 Chancellor Vranitsky announced that the government would decide on the EU question in 1989 and that a membership application had not been ruled out so long as its neutrality position could be reserved.

Switzerland

Swiss policy towards the EU, like Austria's was largely determined by its need to sustain its neutrality policy whilst ensuring market access to the EU. Its central position controlling a large proportion of the EU's transalpine traffic gave it a strong interest in the internal market whilst reinforcing its determination to protect its environmental interests. However, unlike in the Austrian case, Swiss definitions of sovereignty, linked to its highly devolved, direct democracy system of decision-making, put tighter constraints on the possibility of EU membership. The Swiss had always preferred bilateral negotiations with the EU, in which detailed reciprocal rights and duties could be specified. However they were willing to support EFTA initiatives towards the EU so long as they could retain the right to opt out of any parts of a global agreement that might be concluded in the future.

1989 - 1994: The EEA and the search for a new partnership

A possible answer to Wijkman's question concerning institutional harmonisation had been provided by Jacques Delors. In January 1989 Delors gave a speech to the European Parliament (EP) in which he proposed a more 'structured partnership' between the EU and EFTA.[10] Two options were available to EFTA, either they could continue with the piecemeal Luxembourg process and incrementally create a pan-European free trade area, or they could adopt a more ambitious plan, possibly involving a customs union. In terms of institutional structures Delors offered the possibility of either joint institutions or a 'twin pillars' approach, the latter being his preferred option.

The Delors speech was welcomed by EFTA Ministers meeting in Oslo in March 1989 and marked a decisive turning point in EU/EFTA relations. Although the options he presented were only loosely drawn, the EFTA countries were ready for a more active engagement with the EU, indeed Delors' speech was partly based on informal discussions he had already had with the Norwegian Prime Minister Mrs Bruntlund.

From the EU's perspective the proposal formed part of a more wide ranging reappraisal of the EU's external relations. During this period the Community was preoccupied with meeting its 1992 deadline for achieving the internal market and with pressing ahead with proposals for economic and monetary union. A clear priority was therefore given to its deepening agenda. At the same time major changes in eastern Europe were underway which required an active response from the EU. By 1989 the EU's agenda was becoming dangerously overcrowded.

The EEA proposal can therefore be seen as an attempt by the Commission, supported by the French and German governments, to develop a 'variable geometry' model of partnership with groups of countries building a Europe of 'concentric circles'.[11] The first circle around the core would consist of EFTA countries who were economically well prepared to participate in the internal market but were unwilling to accept the EU's finalised politique, whilst the outer circle would consist of predominantly east European countries with weaker economies less willing or able to face the demands of either full EU or EEA membership.

Widening and deepening

Attempts to reconcile deepening with widening have characterised the EU's development since the first enlargement.[12] Discussions of differentiated integration were prevalent in the early 1980s during the Community's Mediterranean enlargement.[13] These focused on both the degree of policy convergence necessary between the EU and potential applicants before enlargement was a realistic possibility, and on the kind of institutional framework most appropriate to ensure that this took place.

Wallace characterised three scenarios for the development of EU relations with its neighbours in 1989. The first, 'looser and wider', would have involved abandoning all proposals for deepening in favour of a looser pan-European framework. The second, 'completion and widening without deepening', would have involved completing the 1992 project, abandoning EMU, and preparing for an early EFTA enlargement. The third, 'consolidation and partnership', would have involved moving on to EMU and developing a new global agreement with EFTA.[14]

Delors' EEA proposal implied a preference for the third scenario. The Delors Group had already started work in 1988 on EMU and was due to report in April 1989. The EEA initiative was a way of keeping the momentum of deepening whilst postponing enlargement.[15] Whether the EEA proposal was intended to be a temporary expedient, to buy the Commission some time, or a permanent feature of the EU's architecture is an open question.

From EFTA's perspective the Delors proposal presented both opportunities and challenges. The EEA proposal offered a more privileged form of partnership than it had before. Faced with the mass of emerging internal market legislation, the limitations of the Luxembourg process were becoming ever clearer. EFTA governments were under considerable pressure from their domestic corporate interests to find an effective form of participation in the new market building process. Yet Delors' preference for a 'two pillars' approach, implying that EFTA's institutional structure and decision-making system would have to more closely resemble the EU's, fundamentally challenged the loose intergovernmental character of EFTA. Although the EFTA response to the Delors proposal was broadly positive, they were not as yet willing to give a clear answer to the question posed earlier by Wijkman. Furthermore, EFTA's credibility as a negotiating bloc was partly compromised by the Austrian government's decision to submit a formal application for EU membership. The application, submitted in July 1989, signalled the Austrians' intention of pursuing a 'twin track' approach, preferring full membership, if available, but accepting the EEA framework as a second best alternative. Whilst the Austrians had never concealed their preference from their fellow EFTA countries, it nevertheless exposed the lack of coherence in EFTA's strategy.

Moving towards negotiations

Following the Oslo meeting a series of working groups was established in order to explore how Delors' proposal might be developed. These groups

24 *The 1995 enlargement of the European Union*

examined the core internal market legislation (the 'four freedoms'), 'flanking' and 'horizontal' policy issues, 'cohesion' issues, and institutional and legal questions. In October 1989 the HLSG reported that '…sufficient common ground has been identified to envisage the possibility of global negotiations between the Community on the one hand and EFTA acting as one, on the other hand, leading to an overall EU/EFTA agreement'.[16]

EFTA saw the acceptance of the internal market *acquis* as the basis for negotiations as a major concession and sought significant influence over future legislation in return. This was always likely to be a difficult challenge to the negotiators given the EU's commitment to the Interlaken principles. The HLSG report noted a number of options for decision-making and reiterated the model of separate EU and EFTA pillars between which there would be 'reciprocal osmosis' during the 'decision shaping' phase. However at this early stage there was no discussion as to how this osmosis would take place.

In December EU and EFTA ministers agreed to open negotiations in the first half of 1990 on the basis of the HLSG report. Negotiations got underway in the spring of 1990 when officials started to identify the areas for serious negotiations. Initially EFTA members claimed a whole series of special interests for which they hoped to get exemptions within the overall agreement. The Swiss adopted the hardest line over decision-making asking for the right of co-decision in EEA legislation in order to preserve their direct democracy system. The free movement of persons was deemed to be especially sensitive, given that 15 per cent of residents and 25 per cent of workers were non-Swiss, including 600,000 Community citizens.[17] They were also concerned about Alpine transit arrangements, as were the Austrians.

For Iceland anxieties focused on fisheries which provided the bulk of the country's hard currency earnings. Norway had similar concerns, together with fears about the possible removal of restrictions on the foreign ownership of natural resources. Finnish concerns centred on the possible foreign ownership of their forestry resources. Whilst the EFTA governments all had political problems with aspects of the *acquis*, they all recognised that some degree of domestic deregulation was necessary to ensure the competitiveness of their economies. Despite their high propensity to invest abroad and their high level of trade interdependency with the EU, most EFTA economies still retained extensive restrictions on their domestic economies into the mid-1980s. These restrictions included limitations on the level of foreign ownership of shares, and corporate cross share holdings, making hostile bids virtually impossible. Most EFTA countries also retained import restrictions on categories of sensitive products, such as some foodstuffs, pharmaceuticals, and most particularly alcoholic beverages.[18]   The EEA therefore proved to be a useful framework for dismantling these restrictions and confronting the domestic interest groups that defended them.

Accommodating these special interests into a coherent negotiating position proved to be very difficult for EFTA, given that the two pillars approach necessitated them coming to a common position. Although aspects of the *acquis* were clearly going to challenge the negotiators, by early 1990 there were already signs that institutional and decision-making issues would be the most problematic. In January Jacques Delors had again spoken to the EP and had indicated that any agreement must stop short of joint decision-making. The EP also indicated that it would not accept an agreement that gave EFTA countries more influence in the process than the EP itself. These views were linked to the fear that wider political changes in eastern Europe might have the effect of diluting the achievements of European integration, particularly by refocusing the attention of Germany.[19]   The ambiguity implicit in the EEA's distinction between decision-making and decision-shaping led to a restatement of the Community orthodoxy.

Formal negotiations start

Following the Commission's submission of a draft mandate to the Council in May, which restated that there should be no compromising the Community's decision-making autonomy, formal negotiations commenced in June. The first phase in the autumn of 1990 concentrated on defining the relevant *acquis*, and on EFTA's requests for permanent derogations. These were strongly resisted by the EU side, and were withdrawn by EFTA on condition that the EU accepted a genuine common decision-making mechanism. In October the EU accepted that institutional and legal questions should be taken in parallel with negotiations on the *acquis*. This reflected heightened anxiety within the EU that failure to meet any of EFTA's concerns would most likely lead to a number of applications for full membership, particularly since in December the Swedish Parliament had given the government a mandate to apply for EU membership.

The joint ministerial meeting on 19 December saw some progress on institutional questions. It was agreed that decisions at EEA level would be taken by consensus with EFTA speaking with one voice implying no opt outs. The EU accepted EFTA's plan for an EEA Council to oversee the development of the Agreement, and for a joint body responsible for its implementation and operation. In May 1991 the joint ministerial meeting found a solution to the problem of the judicial mechanism. EFTA had wanted an independent judicial body to oversee the EEA, whilst the EU had wanted to give this role to the EU's Court of Justice (ECJ). The compromise solution involved a mixed court, independent from, but closely linked to the ECJ, with judges from EFTA and the ECJ. Although at that stage politically acceptable to both sides the model still required further substantial work. In return for this the EFTA countries assured the EU that they would introduce domestic legislation giving supremacy to EEA law where these conflicted with domestic laws. This in effect conceded the supremacy of EU rules over EFTA countries' own, a vital principle that all along EFTA had been extremely reluctant to give ground on. The EU rejected EFTA's demand that individual countries should be able to opt out of EEA rules, a right that had been firmly resisted within the EU.

Three areas still remained unresolved, fisheries, cohesion spending and transit. The first two in particular were closely linked. Spain, which itself had experienced very tough bargaining during its own accession negotiations, was determined to obtain better access to Norwegian and Icelandic waters as its price for agreeing to any EEA deal. Meetings in June failed to finalise the fisheries dossier. On 1 July the Swedish Government submitted its application for EU membership. This reminded the other EFTA countries of the danger of further EFTA fragmentation, and the need to conclude an agreement soon.

The agreement was finally concluded on October 1991 after the Commission reduced its demands for access to fishing resources. However, the Commission also put EFTA under intense pressure and reminded them that the EU's priorities were changing, with more emphasis being given to eastern Europe, should they fail to agree quickly.

Financial transfers agreed at the meeting amounted to ECU 1.5m in soft loans and ECU 500m in grants for environmental and educational projects in Spain, Portugal, Greece and Ireland. On transit, the agreement allowed the Swiss to maintain their 28 ton weight limit, with some heavier trucks allowed through under exceptional circumstances. For Austria the EU agreed 1.3m transit licenses, frozen at that level except for Greece which would get a 29 per cent increase.

European Court of Justice opinion

The complexity of the proposals for the legal enforcement of the EEA Agreement had given cause for concern from the outset of the negotiations. Reconciling legal homogeneity within the EEA without unilaterally extending the power of the ECJ was never going to be straightforward. Indeed in early 1990, when examining the EEA proposal the House of Lords EU Select Committee had commented that 'whatever option is chosen, it would be wise to ensure that the European Court itself is given every opportunity to comment'.[20]

Following the political agreement on the EEA the ECJ's opinion on the draft treaty was sought. In a lengthy opinion of 14 December 1991 the Court ruled that the Agreement was contrary to EU law, identifying a number of fundamental flaws in the way powers were allocated to the proposed EEA Court. The essence of the Court's opinion was that the role of the EEA Court in determining EEA rules throughout the whole EEA would conflict with the ECJ's exclusive competence to interpret EU law under Article 164 of the Treaties. The opinion identified the different objectives of the EEA Treaty and the Treaty of Rome. The EEA Court, it argued, only has to 'ensure the sound operation of rules on free trade and competition under an international treaty which creates obligations only between the contracting parties'.[21] 'In contrast', it continued, 'the Court of Justice has to secure observance of a particular legal order and to foster its development with a view to achieving the objectives set out in .. the EU Treaty. In that context, free trade and competition are merely means of achieving those objectives'.[22]

The opinion added: 'consequently, depending on whether they are sitting on the Court of Justice or on the EEA Court, the judges of the Court of Justice who are members of the EEA Court will have to apply and interpret the same provisions but using different approaches, methods and concepts in order to take into account the nature of each treaty and its particular objectives'.[23]

The opinion also pointed out the contradictory effects of the allocation of powers between the Courts. Interpretations of the agreement by the ECJ requested by national courts in EFTA countries would not be binding on those EFTA courts, though they would be in EU member states.[24] The Court's opinion was a major obstacle to the conclusion of the EEA agreement. By exposing the fundamental flaw at the heart of the whole EEA concept it risked the treaty being seen in the EFTA states as not worth the trouble, particularly as the debate on full membership was gathering momentum in most EFTA countries. In January 1992 the Finnish government sought approval from the Parliament and, in February submitted an application for full EU membership. During 1990 and 1991 it had been looking for ways to reconcile its neutrality policy with the increasing pressure for membership. Given the value placed on Nordic cooperation, the Swedish decision to apply in July 1991 put pressure on the Finns. The election of ultra nationalist deputies in the Russian elections in the autumn of 1991 evoked historical fears about Finnish national security, and proved decisive in moving opinion to the EU membership option. Though not constrained by the neutrality issue, the Norwegians, for domestic political reasons, did not apply for EU membership until November 1992.

In February 1992 a compromise solution to the legal impasse created by the ECJ was found, which involved dropping the idea of a separate EEA Court and involved EFTA setting up its own surveillance mechanism and court mirroring the EU's. Where the application of the rules varied between the EU and EFTA, a committee of officials from both sides would try and resolve the dispute. If this failed the ECJ would be asked for a binding decision. Whilst the solution increased the domestic political acceptability of the EEA in some EFTA countries, by removing the direct interference of the ECJ, it still accepted that in the majority of cases ECJ case law would prevail. The redrafted agreement was accepted by the ECJ.

On 6 December 1992 the Swiss rejected the EEA Treaty by a narrow majority (50.3 per cent). This led to some re-negotiation, in particular the demand from the EU side that the loss of Switzerland's contribution to the EEA's financial mechanism should be made up by the other six EFTA countries. Following a compromise that the interest subsidy granted on the soft loans would be reduced, the agreement was concluded in February 1993, with the treaty coming into force on 1 January 1994.

Outcome of the negotiations

The eventual outcome of the treaty negotiations involved compromises on both sides. However, given the original bargaining positions of the EU and EFTA, arguably EFTA gave more ground. EFTA had initially wanted to take the *acquis communautaire* as the starting point for negotiations, and had requested a series of opt-outs in areas of domestic political sensitivity. The EU maintained that the homogeneity of the *acquis* was inviolable, and that only temporary derogations, reinforced with general safeguard clauses, were acceptable. In this respect the EEA negotiations more closely resembled the 'classical' Community method of full accession negotiations, than intergovernmental treaty bargaining.[25]

For most areas two year transitional periods were applied, though Switzerland was offered five years to implement the free movement of persons legislation. EFTA's higher exhaust emission standards for cars would remain for two years pending the EU's review of its own standards. For fisheries products, EFTA countries were granted limited access to the EU market according to a categorisation of 'sensitivity'. The EU received full market access (with some derogations for Finland, Sweden, Switzerland and Liechtenstein) for fishing products. The EU's share of total allowable catches was raised, with Norway ceding additional 'cohesion cod' to Spain and Portugal.

EFTA also undertook to implement the EU's regime on competition and state aids which in some sectors, such as fisheries, shipbuilding and energy, were extensive and potentially trade distorting. A separate agreement with Switzerland and Austria on transit traffic allowed the Swiss to retain its 28 ton limit but introduce a quota for heavier trucks.

The Agreement also removed restrictions on capital movements. With limited restrictions, similar to those in Denmark, allowed on the foreign purchase of second homes, the EFTA countries removed all constraints on inward direct investment, equity participation and real estate purchase. The free movement of services, including the right of establishment, was extended throughout the whole EEA. The free movement of persons, including the mutual recognition of professional qualifications was also applied.

EFTA linked acceptance of the *acquis* to its demands for satisfactory legal and institutional mechanisms. Arguably EFTA did not achieve this objective.[26] Although EFTA obtained a right of information and consultation for internal market legislation and a collective right of opt-out, EFTA cannot stop the EU from introducing new legislation. The individual right of opt-out demanded by the Swiss was not accepted. Thus, although the degree of decision-shaping accorded to EFTA is more extensive than that granted to any other non EU associate, it nevertheless stops short of real decision-making powers. Despite the tortuous negotiations, the Interlaken Principles prevailed. The establishment of an EFTA surveillance authority (ESA), with similar powers to those of the Commission, to ensure compliance with the Agreement, particularly in relation to competition policy, was a de facto acceptance by EFTA of both the supremacy of the content of EU law and supranationality in its implementation.

Operation of the EEA

The operation of the EEA regime has born out many of the concerns voiced during its negotiation.   In practice it has proved difficult to reconcile EFTA's need for active involvement in the decision-making process with the preservation of the EU's autonomy.   Concerns have focused on four main areas.[27]   First, the operation of the two pillar structure has proved to be opaque and cumbersome.   Where additional legislation has needed to be adopted by the EEA Joint Committee, the Commission has had to play an ambiguous role as arbiter of the relevant EEA legislation, as the representative of EFTA in the EU Council's working groups, and as the Council's negotiator in the EEA Joint Committee.   Second, the overall dependence of EFTA on the Commission has created difficulties.   Delays have occurred in the Joint Committee, for instance when legislation is still being consolidated, or where member states have argued that its extension to EFTA might affect the implementation of legislation.   Third, problems have arisen during the decision shaping phase of the EEA process.   EFTA's participation in Comitology Committees has been circumscribed to the minimum allowed in the agreement.   Beyond this initial stage EFTA states have had to rely on informal channels of influence, through EU member states and the EP.   Fourth, enforcement cooperation has been limited.   Obtaining information concerning technical barriers to trade within the EU has sometimes been difficult for ESA.   New developments in regulatory policy, for instance concerning state aids to airlines have been difficult for ESA to input.

   Yet despite its limitations the EEA served two important purposes, in facilitating the administrative learning process in preparation for full membership, and in catalysing the domestic reform process in the EFTA states.   The EEA required the EFTA states to set up cross-ministerial groups to coordinate policy and to reorientate their domestic policy processes to comply with EU norms.   Though the formal channels of consultation were limited in the EEA, the experience of finding informal ways round its limitations was a useful introduction to the realities of full EU membership.

   The EEA was also critical in speeding up the process of domestic deregulation which gathered momentum during the late 1980s.   For instance the influential 1993 report of the Swedish Royal Commission on Economic Reform (The Lindbeck Report) argued strongly in favour of implementing EU legislation, even if the EEA was delayed.   Business groups in EFTA saw the EEA as a way of holding the EU responsible for internal policy reforms which they considered desirable, even if painful to implement.   As Smith has concluded:

> The significance of the EEA lay in its ability to act as a transitory framework for catalysing political alignments both in the context of existing domestic programmes of regulatory reform, and in the context of the pre-accession strategies of four EFTA states.   In both cases the agreement overlay an alignment of domestic interests which was highly conducive to a process of harmonisation based asymmetrically on internal market rules.[28]

Conclusion

As an exercise in the creation of variable geometry the EEA is of limited value.   The experience of trying to reconcile active participation in the EU without membership ultimately proved fruitless, and suggests that both the EU and its potential members need to confront the full implications of enlargement sooner rather than later.   Though there are significant differences between EFTA and the central and east European countries (CEEC's), there are indications that some of the lessons of the EEA have been learnt by both parties.   The CEEC's have made full membership their overriding priority, whilst the EU is developing a 'pre-accession strategy' which supports the transition process in eastern Europe, but does not promise full participation until membership is achieved.   Whilst some measure of differentiation may be conceded on the way to the next enlargement, this is only acceptable because the objective is not in doubt. So long as the EU continues to exercise such a magnetic attraction to its neighbours, full membership of the club, with all its costs and benefits will remain the preferred option.

Bibliography

Bruntlund, G.H. (1988), 'Norway, the EC and European Cooperation', *Office of the Prime Minister*, Oslo.
Camps, M. (1964), *Britain and the European Community 1955-1964*, Oxford University Press, Oxford.
Charlton, M. (1983), *The Price of Victory*, BBC, London.
Delors, J. (1989), *Debates of the European Parliament 1988-89 Session*, Proceedings from 16-20 January 1989.
European Court of Justice (1991), *Opinion of the Court on the draft agreement between the Community and EFTA relating to the creation of the EEA*, Opinion 1/91, 14 December 1991.
EC Commission (1989), *Commission communication to the Council on the future relationship between the Community and EFTA*, November 1989.
EFTA (1988), *EFTA Trade*, 1988 Economic Affairs Department, EFTA, Geneva.
EFTA (1992), *State Aids in EFTA in 1990*, 5th Annual Report by the Secretariat, Geneva.
Government of Sweden (1987), *Proposition 1987/88:66*, Stockholm.
House of Commons (1990), *Trade with EFTA*, Trade and Industry Committee, Session 1989-90, 4th Report.
House of Lords (1990), *Relations between the Community and EFTA*, Select Committee on the EC Session 1989-90, 14th Report.
Pedersen, T. (1994), *European Union and the EFTA Countries*, Pinter, London.
Preston, C. (1995), 'Obstacles to EU enlargement', *Journal of Common Market Studies*, vol. 33, no. 3 September 1995.
Smith, E. (1995), *The European Economic Area as a Transitory Regime*, Sussex European Institute, September 1995.
Tsalicoglou, I. (1995), *Negotiating for entry*, Dartmouth, Aldershot.
Wallace, H. (1985), *Europe: the Challenge of Diversity*, Royal Institute of International Affairs, London.
Wallace, H. (1989), *Widening and Deepening: the European Community and the New European Agenda*, Royal Institute of International Affairs, London.
Wijkman, P. (1989), *Exploring the European Economic Space*, EFTA, Bulletin 1/1989.
Wijkman, P. (1990), *Patterns of Production and Trade in Western Europe*, EFTA Occasional Paper, no. 32.

Notes

1. See Camps, M., *Britain and the European Community 1955-1964*, Oxford University Press, Oxford, 1964, and Charlton, M., *The Price of Victory*, BBC, London, 1983.

2. Pedersen, T., *European Union and the EFTA Countries*, Pinter, London, 1994, p. 19.

3. Pedersen, T., *European Union and the EFTA Countries*, op cit, p. 21.

4. Wijkman, P., *Exploring the European Economic Space*, EFTA, Bulletin 1/1989, 1989.

5.   Tsalicoglou, I., *Negotiating for Entry*, Dartmouth, Aldershot, 1995.

6.   Wijkman, P., *Patterns of Production and Trade in Western Europe*, EFTA Occasional Paper, no. 32.

7.   EFTA, *EFTA Trade*, Economic Affairs Department, Geneva, 1988.

8.   Wijkman, P., *Patterns of Production and Trade in Western Europe*, op cit, p. 20.

9.   Bruntland, G.H., *Norway, the EC and European Cooperation*, Office of the Prime Minister, 1988.

10. Delors, J., *Debates of the European Parliament 1988-89 Session*, Proceedings from 16-20 January 1989.

11. Pedersen, T., *European Union and the EFTA Countries*, op cit, p. 34.

12. Preston, C., *Obstacles to EU Enlargement*, Journal of Common Market Studies, vol. 33, no. 3, September 1995.

13. Wallace, H., *Europe: the Challenge of Diversity*, Royal Institute of International Affairs, London, 1985.

14. Wallace, H., *Widening and Deepening: the European Community and the New European Agenda*, Royal Institute of International Affairs, London, 1989.

15. Pedersen, T., *European Union and the EFTA Countries*, op cit.

16. EC Commission, *Commission Communication to the Council on the Future Relationship Between the Community and EFTA*, November 1989.

17. House of Lords, *Relations between the Community and EFTA*, Select Committee on the EC Session 1989-90, 4th Report, p. 35.

18. House of Commons, *Trade with EFTA*, Trade and Industry Committee, Session 1989-90, 4th Report.

19. Pedersen, T., *European Union and the EFTA Countries*, op cit.

20. House of Lords, *Relations between the Community and EFTA*, Select Committee on the EC Session 1989-90, 14th Report, p. 27.

21. European Court of Justice, *Opinion of the Court on the Draft Agreement between the Community and EFTA relating to the creation of the EEA*, Opinion 1/91, 14 December 1991, para 49.

22. European Court of Justice, *Opinion of the Court on the Draft Agreement between the Community and EFTA relating to the Creation of the EEA*, op cit, para 50.

23. European Court of Justice, *Opinion of the Court on the Draft Agreement between the Community and EFTA relating to the Creation of the EEA*, op cit, para 51.

24. European Court of Justice, *Opinion of the Court on the Draft Agreement between the Community and EFTA relating to the creation of the EEA*, op cit, para 62.

25. Preston, C., 'Obstacles to EU Enlargement', op cit.

26. Pedersen, T., *European Union and the EFTA Countries*, op cit, p. 69.

27. Smith, E., *The European Economic Area as a Transitory Regime*, Sussex European Institute, September 1995.

28. *Ibid*, p. 14.

3 The First Enlargement Negotiations of the EU[1]

FRANCISCO GRANELL

The 1995 EU enlargement compared with the previous EU enlargements

European integration has always moved qualitatively and quantitatively in an interrelated process. Qualitatively because the European Community (EC) has developed from the sectorially limited European Coal and Steel Community (ECSC), created by the Paris Treaty on 18 April 1951, to the very ambitious European Union (EU), created by the Treaty on European Union signed in Maastricht on 7 February 1992, - with the two essential intermediate steps of the Rome Treaties signed on 25 March 1957 establishing the European Economic Community (EEC) and the EURATOM - the Single European Act (SEA) signed in Luxembourg on 17 February 1986 and in The Hague on 28 February 1986, and with a large amount of secondary legislation and judgements of the European Court of Justice (ECJ) constantly deepening the European integration.

Quantitatively because the six ECSC, EC and EURATOM founding members (Belgium, France, Germany, Italy, Luxembourg and the Netherlands) became nine from 1 January 1973 (with the accession of Denmark, Ireland and the United Kingdom [UK]), 10 from 1 January 1981 (with the accession of Greece), 12 from 1 January 1986 (with the accession of Portugal and Spain) and 15 since 1 January 1995 (with the accession of Austria, Finland and Sweden). In the meantime - on 1 October 1990 - a 'sui generis' enlargement took place: the full and instantaneous integration of the länder of the former German Democratic Republic as a result of German reunification.

Frequently during the qualitative process of deepening European integration, and the quantitative process of successive enlargements, some observers expressed concern about the difficulty of carrying out the one process alongside the other.   In fact, European integration has made significant advances on both fronts, through the leadership of some of the new Member States, in the definition of new European law and policies. Moreover, even if applicant countries are requested to accept the *acquis communautaire* in full, as a precondition for full membership, enlargement negotiations have played a substantial role in the creation of the EU as we know it today, by incorporating new views and leadership to the integration process.

Negotiations for the most recent enlargement of the EU started in February 1993 and can be said to have finished either in February 1994 or on 1 January 1995 with the implementation of the Accession Documents for Austria, Finland and Sweden and the non-accession of Norway.

Negotiations which took Spain and Portugal more than six years, Greece two years and ten months, and nineteen months in the case of the UK, Denmark and Ireland were completed in little over twelve months for Austria, Finland and Sweden (Table 3.1).

Table 3.1 Accessions to the EU and current requests for membership

COUNTRIES	REQUEST FOR ACCESSION	COMMISSION'S OPINION	OPENING OF ACCESSION NEGOTIATI- ONS	ACCESSION TREATY	FULL MEMBERSHIP
Britain	10.05.1967 (1)	}	}	}	}
Denmark	11.05.1967	} 29.09.1967	} 30.06.1970	} 22.01.1972	} 01.01.1973
Ireland	11.05.1967	}	}	}	}
Norway	21.07.1967	}	}	}	} (2)
Greece	12.06.1975	29.01.1976	27.07.1976	28.05.1979	01.01.1981
Portugal	28.03.1977	19.05.1978	17.10.1978	}	} 01.01.1986
Spain	28.07.1977	29.11.1978	05.02.1979	} 12.06.1985	} 01.01.1986
Turkey	14.04.1987	14.12.1989	-	-	
Austria	17.07.1989	01.08.1991	01.02.1993	24.06.1994	01.01.1995
Cyprus	04.07.1990	30.06.1993	-	-	
Malta	16.07.1990	30.06.1993	-	-	
Sweden	01.07.1991	31.07.1992	01.02.1993	24.06.1994	01.01.1995
Finland	18.03.1992	04.11.1992	01.02.1993	24.06.1994	01.01.1995
Switzerland	26.05.1992	(3)	-	-	
Norway	25.11.1992	24.03.1993	05.04.1993	24.06.1994	(4)
Hungary	01.04.1994	-			
Poland	08.04.1994	-			

(1)   Previously there had been an initial request which General De Gaulle vetoed on 14 January, 1963.
(2)   Except for Norway which, by a referendum on 24 September, 1972, decided not to become a member.
(3)   No further developments expected after the Swiss "No" referendum on EEA on 12 December, 1992.
(4)   Norwegians rejected membership in the referendum of 28 November 1994.

This 1995 EU Enlargement exercise is the Community's fourth (or fifth if we include the absorption of East Germany), and is supposed to be the last before the revolution of the 1996 Intergovernmental Conference (IGC) that will modify some of the rules originally created to run a Community of six thereby enabling the EU to expand to a dozen additional members.

The 1995 solely quantitative enlargement

The 1995 accession of Austria, Finland and Sweden is the last solely quantitative enlargement in the European process of integration, because the three new members are upper-income countries able to fully participate in the EU's *acquis* with only minor technical and quantitative adaptations.

Future enlargements, after the 1996 IGC, will necessarily be qualitative in the sense that a merely formal quantitative transposition of legislation will not be enough to achieve the desired economic impact or to ensure that the internal market continues to function effectively. If, until now, the three previous quantitative enlargements of the EU had taken place by virtue of article 98 of the ECSC Treaty, article 237 of the EEC Treaty and article 205 of the EURATOM Treaty, the 1995 quantitative enlargement from 12 to 15 was based on article 'O' of the Treaty of Maastricht creating the EU.

This chapter makes it clear that the Union is open to any European country interested in joining and ready to accept the European *acquis*. This implies that the 1995 enlargement included the acceptance by the candidate countries not only of the traditional EU *acquis* but also of the extensions provided for in the SEA (which created the Single Market) and the Treaty on European Union (TEU), and this means that new members have had to accept the EU's *acquis* in its entirety:

- the institutional provisions: governing intergovernmental and supranational EU bodies, their composition and interactions with the logical numerical adaptations;
- the legal framework: the different kinds of Community treaties, regulations, acts and other texts;
- the financial regulations establishing the Union's budgetary resources and expenses, the European Development Fund (EDF) and the European Investment Bank (EIB) by-laws;
- the norms establishing the free circulation of goods, persons and capital inside the EU, the freedom to provide services and the freedom of establishment;
- the common Community rules and standards concerning approximation of laws, fair competition and monopolies, indirect taxation, veterinary and plant health, commercial law, etc.;
- the common policies: Common Agricultural Policy (CAP); Common External Tariff and Commercial Policy; Development Policy; Regional, Social and Cohesion Policy; Transport Policy and Trans-European

Networks; Consumer and Health Protection, Research and Information policies, Education, Statistics, Energy Policy; Fisheries Policy; Industrial Policy;

- Economic and Monetary Union (EMU) as a further stage of the European Monetary System;
- The so-called new 'pillars' of the TEU;
- The Common Foreign and Security Policy (CFSP);
- Cooperation in the fields of Justice and Home Affairs;
- The rights and duties derived from the concept of 'citizenship of the Union' included in the first pillar of the Maastricht Treaty.

The mechanical adaptation of members' voting rights, an increase in the number of Parliamentarians (an increase of 59 to a total of 626 whereby Austria will designate 21, Sweden 22 and Finland 16), Commissioners (from 17 to 20) and other institutions' members, official languages and several lists of secondary legislation are the only permanent modifications incorporated by the 1995 enlargement of the EU to the previous *acquis*.

The negotiation process

The first mention of the possibility of a fourth enlargement, in accordance with the openness established by article 'O' of the TEU, was made by the EU's European Council held in Maastricht (December 1991). At that meeting the Commission received the mandate to prepare a Report concerning this issue to be presented to the Council to be held in Lisbon in June 1992. After examination of this Report entitled 'The Challenge of Enlargement', the Lisbon Council decided that official negotiations with those EFTA countries wishing to become members of the Union would begin immediately after the ratification of the TEU and an agreement on the Delors II financial package had been reached; saying that 'this enlargement is possible on the basis of the institutional provisions contained in the Treaty on the Union and the attached declarations' (on the number of members of the Commission and the European Parliament [EP]). At that stage, Austria, Sweden, Finland and Switzerland had applied for membership, and an application from Norway was anticipated (finally arriving in November 1992). All these countries were expected to participate in the EEA when it started (initially set for 1 January 1993 and then postponed to 1 January 1994).

In fact, most of EFTA's members had decided to apply for membership in the expectation that integration with the EU would make it easier for them to cope with internal problems rather than being left out. At the same time, they were interested in participating in the decision-making process of the Union and having influence within the Community as equal partners rather than being passively subjected to the impact of EU rules through the EEA.

As is already well known, at the heart of the EEA was the idea of enabling the Community's EFTA neighbours to enjoy the benefits of the EU's post-1992 Single European Market (SEM). In return, the EFTA states would accept the rules of the single market. The EEA Oporto Treaty signed on 2 May 1992 - amended by the Brussels Protocol of 17 March 1993 after the non-accession of Switzerland and in force from 1 January 1994 - established:

- abolition of customs duties and quantitative restrictions in trade in industrial goods;
- free movement of people;
- free movement of capital;
- free movement of services;
- EFTA countries also taking over EU competition rules and creating an independent EFTA surveillance authority and an EFTA court;
- technical barriers to trade being removed, but, as free movement applies only to goods originating within the EEA, border controls between EU and EFTA countries could not therefore be removed;
- special arrangements on fisheries and agricultural products;
- discriminatory restrictions having to be abolished;
- a financial mechanism to reduce regional disparities, with a view to ensuring an overall balance of benefits for developing zones of the EU, being established;
- participation of EFTA countries in some EU 'flanking' and horizontal policies: research & technological development, information services, consumer protection, audio-visual, etc.;
- common EU/EFTA organs being created.

With all these regulations created by the EEA Agreement, it was clear that the EFTA countries accepted a substantial part of the EU-*acquis* when they signed the EEA Agreement. It is precisely for that reason that a distinction was made between the EFTA candidates and other countries in the text of the Lisbon European Council's conclusions (June 1992).

To facilitate a fast track process, the Lisbon Council decided that the EFTA enlargement should be made within the framework of existing institutional regulations; reform would only be a condition for future new enlargements. The framework for the EFTA negotiations established in November 1992 comprised an indicative list of negotiating chapters (Table 3.2), in which subjects included under chapters 1 to 11 of the list had been negotiated in depth for the purposes of the Treaty of the EEA. This simplified the accession negotiations. Chapters 12 to 16 were only partially included in the EEA, while chapters 17 to 22 dealt with EU policies not covered by the EEA. Chapters 23 to 26 - except for the EMS and ERM of chapter 23 - referred to new elements introduced by the Maastricht Treaty; the rest were of a more general nature.

Table 3.2 Accession negotiations' chapter headings

Chapters almost fully covered by the EEA	1. Free movement of goods 2. Freedom to provide services and right of establishment 3. Freedom of movement for workers 4. Free movement of capital 5. Transport policy 6. Competition policy 7. Consumers and health protection 8. Research and information technologies 9. Education 10. Statistics 11. Company law
Chapters only partly covered	12. Social policy 13. Environment 14. Energy 15. Agriculture 16. Fisheries
Chapters in areas covered by EU but not covered by EEA	17. Customs union 18. External relations 19. Structural instruments 20. Regional policy 21. Industrial policy 22. Taxation
Areas introduced by Maastricht Treaty	23. Economic and monetary union (*) 24. Foreign and security policy 25. Justice and home affairs 26. Other provisions
General chapters	27. Financial and budgetary provisions 28. Institutions 29. Other

(*) Chapter partially covered as EU *Acquis* through the European Monetary System.

The idea of a 'fast track' was also motivated by the EU's need to give a quick concrete response to concerns expressed by the EFTA countries regarding the need to participate in a 'political Europe' as a result of German reunification.

But despite the EEA negotiations having helped to accelerate accession talks, it was clear that the degree of progress towards European integration since the Portuguese and Spanish enlargement of 1986 had created many additional issues that had to be considered. Hence these enlargement negotiations would be more complex than previous EU enlargement negotiations. These issues included:

- the introduction of the Single Market by the Twelve at the beginning of 1993 now meant that there could be no internal frontiers and border controls;
- the introduction of the new pillars of Maastricht: CFSP and cooperation on Justice and Home Affairs, plus additional elements such as citizenship of the Union;
- EMU, on top of the EMS and ERM.

At the same time, the new European environment that followed the collapse of the Berlin Wall had introduced new parameters to the negotiations. It was perhaps because of this new wider framework that, initially, it seemed likely that CFSP would cause some difficulties for the three neutral candidates (Austria, Sweden, Finland). However, they were to finally agree to subscribe fully to the objectives and contents of the new pillars.

Negotiations were more difficult concerning those EU chapters not covered by the EEA Agreement: agriculture, regional policy, transport (mainly for Austria), environmental questions, and fisheries (only for Norway). At the same time, although if it was not a problem between the Union and the four candidates but a problem among the Twelve and for the EP, a solution to the institutional question (qualified majority) remained one of the most serious obstacles to a conclusion of the negotiations. These negotiations were not like those for the EEA. In the latter, the EFTA countries established a joint position in order to negotiate as one with the EU Commission (entrusted with a negotiating mandate by the Council). In the former, the fact that there were four parallel sets of negotiations between each candidate and the Council of Ministers - supported by the Commission - illustrated that the negotiations were of an intergovernmental nature.

The individual admissibility of each candidate country had been previously analyzed in four Commission Opinions. Groundwork carried out during the preparation of these Opinions helped to define the factors affecting admission, since each Opinion contained a detailed analysis of the consequences of accession for each applicant country gave an indication of the sectors where problems were to be expected. The preparation of these Opinions required 24 months for Austria, 12 months for Sweden, 7 months for Finland and 4 months for Norway. The December 1992 Edinburgh European Council, having taken account of all these practical considerations, the agreement on the EU's future financing (the Delors II package) and the prospects for early ratification of the Treaty of Maastricht creating the EU, subsequently agreed that enlargement negotiations with the EFTA applicants would start at the beginning of 1993. On the basis of the Commission's Opinions and the above mentioned decisions, the opening ministerial session of the Accession negotiations for Austria, Sweden and Finland took place on 1 February 1993; these were televised, reflecting the EU's policy of greater openness. Meanwhile, the opening ministerial session for Norway took place on 5 April 1993.

From the outset, the negotiations were conducted in the form of four intergovernmental conferences between the Twelve and the candidate countries by the Council of Ministers, with the help of the Commission which had created for this purpose an Enlargement Task Force at its meeting of 22 January 1993. The GISELA (*Groupe Interservice d'Elargissement*) network, comprising experts from all the Commission Directorates General (DGs), was also actively involved. The existence of these four parallel negotiations, together with the political will on both sides, created a kind of competition, with candidates vying with each other to maximize their national interests and to obtain more concessions while trying to keep ahead. This created a special dynamism in which the Enlargement Task Force, various Commission DGs, the Council Secretariat, the Presidency, the Troika and Candidates were involved.

To enable the negotiations to progress in an orderly way, provision was made, where possible, to hold parallel meetings for each candidate country at ministerial and deputy levels. The rotating Presidency of the Council (Denmark then Belgium in 1993, Greece the first half of 1994) determined the dates and agendas for the negotiations in collaboration with the applicant countries, while the Secretariat General of the Council established a special team for the preparation and drafting of the Conferences' conclusions.

The negotiations had as their objective the creation of transitional periods to allow for the incorporation of the *acquis communautaire* into the legislation of the new Member States and the authorization of certain temporary derogations. In some cases, 'imaginative' solutions were necessary: the 'third option' for avoiding frustration on environmental issues, the creation of the new regional policy Objective 6 for Arctic areas with a low-density population, etc. However, it was sometimes negotiations among the Twelve themselves, in order to define a common negotiating position vis-à-vis the four applicants, and the way that each candidate country presented the negotiations back home, with a view to obtaining favourable results in the forthcoming referendum on EU membership and in imminent domestic general elections (Sweden: 18 September 1994, Austria: 9 November, Finland: just after accession), caused more difficulties than the negotiations between the Twelve and the candidate countries. In this context, different negotiating priorities and differences in approach with respect to many of the subjects have been very common.

The Commission services had already indicated in the respective Opinions on the incorporation of each country into the EU, those matters which had to be dealt with in order to limit the problems which each of the Accessions Countries posed. The Commission had also maintained a useful exchange of information of various sorts with the four EFTA countries in the context of the EEA Treaty. During this initial contact, a thorough analysis of the secondary legislation of each candidate country was carried out and exploratory talks were held. The Four then submitted their respective position papers requesting temporary exemptions (permanent ones not being possible), or periods of adaptation to the *acquis*, which they hoped to obtain from the Community institutions in order to have a problem-free integration. On the basis of all this background information, the European Commission prepared draft Common Positions for the Union to reply to the requests of the applicants on each of the contentious subjects. These draft Common Positions were then sent to the Council to be debated in an ad hoc group called 'Enlargement', created in the Council to achieve a common negotiating position for the Twelve vis-à-vis each of the points before the conference where acceptance of the *acquis* would cause difficulties for one or other of the candidate countries. Once a common position was reached at the level of the Twelve (whether it was at the level of the Enlargement Group, of COREPER [Committee of Permanent Representatives] or the General Affairs Ministers at the Council itself), the Common Positions of the Community were given to the candidate countries to be discussed and agreed at deputy level and/or at ministerial level in the Negotiating Conference. Table 3.3 gives a picture of the negotiation process and Table 3.4 a picture of the progress of the accession negotiations from their beginning in February 1993 to their end in March 1994.

Table 3.3 The negotiation process

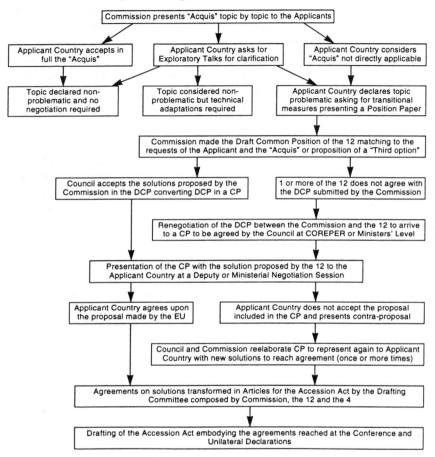

DCP: Draft Common Procedure
CP: Common Position

Successive European Councils requested the Twelve, the European institutions and the four applicant countries to be 'diligent' in the negotiations, in order to incorporate the new members by 1 January 1995. This date was first mentioned in the conclusions of the Copenhagen Summit (21-22 June 1993) while the Brussels Summit (28 December 1993) urged the contracting parties to finalize the negotiations by 1 March 1994. From the beginning, many policymakers considered this date a very ambitious deadline, but everybody involved in the negotiations took it as a challenge.

Table 3.4 Accession negotiation conferences

1993	Ministerial Level	Deputies Level	Decisions taken etc.
1 Feb }	A SF S		} Opening of negotiations.
2 Feb }		1st A 1st SF 1st S	} Agreement on work programme.
11 Mar		1st A	Chaps 8,9,10,11 & 16 declared non-problematic.
11 Mar		2nd SF	Chaps 5,7,8,9,10,11 & 12 declared problematic.
12 Mar		2nd S	Chaps 3,4,8,9,10,11 & 12 declared non-problematic.
5 Apr	N		Opening negotiations.
7 Apr		1st N	Agreement on work programme.
28 May }		3rd A 3rd SF	A agreed to CP on dentists' training (ch.2), female workers & night work (ch.12), employee protection in cases of employer insolvency (ch.12), noise from aeroplanes (ch.13). SF agreed to CPs on safety belts (ch.1), on 3rd Life assurance directive (ch.2) & on direct investment (ch.4).
28 May }		2nd N 3rd S	N agreed to CPs on safety belts (ch.1) & returnable bottles (ch.1). S could not agree to CPs under chaps 1,2 & 13.
8 Jun }	2nd S 2nd SF		Chaps 3,5,7,8,9,10,11 & 13 closed. Chaps 3,5,7,8,9,10,11 & 12 closed.
9 Jun }	2nd A 2nd N		Chaps 7,9,11,12 & 16 closed. Chaps 7,8,9,11 & 12 closed.
22 Jul		4th A	Chaps 3 & 21 declared non-problematic. A agreed to CP on vehicle noise (ch.1) & railways (ch.5).

28 Jul }		4th SF	SF agreed to CPs on definition of vodka (ch.1), Finnish liqueurs (ch.1), radioactive safety standards & health protection (ch.13) & energy stockpiling (ch.14). Chap 21 declared non-problematic.
		3rd N	N agreed to CPs on credit institutions' own funds and third non-life assurance directive (ch.2), advertisements for alcoholic products (ch.2) & titanium dioxide waste (ch.13). Chaps 3 & 10 declared non-problematic.
28 Jul		4th S	SP agreed to CP on third life assurance directive (ch.2). Chap 21 declared non-problematic.
23 Sep		5th S	S agreed (conditionally) to CP on energy (ch.14). Chap 17 declared non-problematic.
29 Sep		5th A	A agreed to CPs on TV broadcasting (ch.2), statistics (ch.10), Chernobyl, EURATOM safety standards, bathing water quality, conservation of wild birds (ch.13) & energy (ch.14).
5 Oct }	3rd A 3rd SF 3rd N 3rd S		} Exchange of views. Chap 14 closed.
4 Nov }		6th A	A agreed to CP on imports from CEECs (ch.18).
		5th SF	SF agreed to CPs on Finnish liqueurs No.2 (ch.1), bathing water quality (ch.13) & customs union (ch.17).
		4th N	N agreed to CP on driving licences (ch.5) & financial & budgetary provisions (ch.27). Chaps 2 & 21 declared non-problematic.
		6th S	Chap 2 declared non-problematic.
9 Nov }	4th A 4th SF 4th N 4th S		} Extension of work programme to include the Maastricht chaps.
25 Nov		6th SF	SF agreed to CPs on financial services (ch.2), statistics (ch.10), radioactive waste & sulphur content of certain fuels (ch.13) & Common Commercial Policy (ch.18).

26 Nov		7th A	A agreed to CP on tobacco monopoly (ch.6).
15 Dec		8th A 7th SF	} Exchange of views.
16 Dec		5th N 7th S	} Exchange of views.
21 Dec }	5th A 5th S 5th N 5th S		A agreed to CPs on MRLs of veterinary medicinal products in foodstuffs of animal origin, light commercial vehicles (ch.1), tobacco monopolies (ch.6), radioactive contamination of foodstuffs, hazardous waste, PCP/PCT, lead & benzine content of petrol, sulphur content of certain fuels (ch.13). Chaps 6,13,24,25 & 26 closed. N agreed to CPs on fiscal incentives in motor vehicle sector (ch.1), hazardous waste & PCB/PCT (ch.13) & Baltic states (ch.18). Chaps 24 & 25 closed. Chaps 6,13,18,24,25 & 26 closed.
1994			
21 Jan }		9th A 8th SF 6th N 8th S	Chaps 2 & 6 closed. Exchange of views. Chap 26 closed. Exchange of views.
3 Feb		10th A	Chaps 8,17 & 18 closed.
8 Feb }	6th A 6th SF 6th N 6th S		Exchange of views. Chap 17 closed. Exchange of views. Chap 17 closed.
17 Feb }		11th A 9th SF 7th N 9th S	Exchange of views. Joint declaration on Nordic cooperation agreed (ch.29). Chaps 4,6 & 18 closed. Joint declaration on Nordic cooperation agreed (ch.29). Joint declaration on Nordic cooperation agreed (ch.29).

22 Feb }	7th A 7th SF 7th N 7th S		Exchange of views. Sf agreed to CP on secondary residences (ch.4), fisheries (ch.16), maritime links (ch.29), Åland Islands (ch.29) & the Sami people (ch.29). N agreed to CP on the Sami people (ch.29). S agreed to CP on the Sami people (ch.29).
1 Mar }	8th A 8th SF 8th S		Agreement on 'transit' & bilateral transport agreements, agricultural agreements, agricultural, regional & budgetary provisions as well as agricultural quotas & veterinary questions. Agreement on Nordic agriculture, regional & budgetary questions, veterinary issues & agricultural quotas. Agreement on budgetary compensations, agriculture, regional & veterinary questions.
8 Mar }	8th N	9th A	Agreement on budgetary compensations, agriculture, regional & veterinary questions. Chaps 2 & 6 closed.
15 Mar	9th N		Agreement on fisheries (ch.14) & EMU (ch.23).
30 Mar }		12th A 10th SF 8th N 10th S	} Final agreement on chaps 23 & 28 & some Declarations.
11/12 Apr }		9th N 11th S 11th SF 13th A	} Acceptance by the candidates of the final texts of the Accession Treaty, Act of Accession, Annexes, Protocols & Final Act to start the signature & ratification procedures.
24 Jun			Signature in Corfu of the Accession Documents by the Heads of Government & other plenipotentiaries of the '12' & of the '4'.

1995			
1 Jan			By written procedure the '15' enlarged Council of Ministers adopts the technical decisions to be taken on account of the non-accession of Norway.

A = Austria   SF = Finland   N = Norway   S = Sweden

CP = Common Position of the EU   chap(s) = chapter(s)

The negotiations were concluded at the political level with Sweden, Finland and Austria on 1 March 1994 and with Norway slightly later on the 16 March 1994, owing to the need to negotiate further on some remaining issues, notably fisheries. Following this political agreement between the Union and the candidates on all points raised by them, the final outstanding chapter, 'Institutions', was settled by the Union at Ionnina on the 27 March 1994; the Four Accession Conferences then agreed on all negotiation chapters on the 30 March. A Drafting Committee - composed of experts from the twelve Member States, the four applicants, the Council's Secretariat and the Commission - subsequently drew up the Accession Treaty and the Act of Accession, its annexes, protocols and appended Declarations. The completed texts were finally accepted in the four final deputies' sessions held on 11 and 12 April 1994.

With the formal positive Commission opinion of 19 April 1994, the EP gave its four positive assents (Legislative Resolutions) in its plenary session held in Strasbourg on 4 May, 1994 after a six-hour debate. It was the first time that the assent procedure of the Maastricht Treaty had been used by the EP in an enlargement context. The assents were granted by huge and unprecedented majorities, more than 100 votes above the required majority (Norway: 376 for, 24 against with 57 abstentions; Austria: 378,24,60; Finland: 377,21,61 and Sweden 381,21,60), thereby confounding pessimistic forecasts. Then, after the positive decision by the Council on 16 May and the approval of the documents concerning the accession by the Governments of the four applicants, the signing ceremony took place on 24 June in Corfu during the Greek European Council.

The Treaty of Accession set out the principle that the four countries, Austria, Finland, Norway and Sweden, would become members of the EU under the material conditions established in the Act of Accession which forms an integral part of the Treaty. The Act of Accession, its annexes and Protocols lay down the principles agreed in the negotiations and enacted the agreed changes to the Treaties where required by the 'quantitative' approach. Annex I contains factual technical adaptations to the Community's secondary legislation (i.e. milk quotas). Other Annexes included temporary derogations as Joint and Unilateral Declarations, Protocols and a Final Act completed the Accession documents.

After the signature, the ratification process for the Sixteen began, in accordance with the respective constitutional requirements. The governments of the four had promised their respective populations a referendum. These were held on 12 June in Austria, 16 October in Finland, 13 November in Sweden and 28 November in Norway. The Austrian referendum resulted in a massive 'yes'-vote of 66.4 per cent. In Finland, the 'yes' vote was 56.9 per cent, while in Sweden the vote was 52 per cent in the affirmative. But the Norwegians rejected EU membership by a slight majority of 52.5 per cent. The result came after a long, hard-fought campaign on an issue that had obsessed Norway for years, since 1972, when 53.5 per cent of the voters rejected membership of what was then the EEC. Opinion polls had placed the 'no' vote well ahead, but the margin narrowed after the 'yes' votes in Finland and Sweden. In light of this rejection, the Twelve, plus the Secretariat of the Council and the Commission, prepared, during December 1994, the decisions to be formally taken by the enlarged Council of Ministers (now fifteen) on 1 January - by written procedure - to adjust the instruments of Accession and the Ionnina institutional compromise to the reality created by Norway's non-accession.

Given the history of intense cooperation between the EU members and the acceding countries (notably through the 1972 FTAs and the EEA Agreement), the integration of the three new member States into the Union's legal and economic system will be more rapid than in previous enlargements. Most of the EU *acquis* applied in the new Member States from the day of accession because the temporary derogations and transitional periods were very limited in scope and quantity. In a number of areas, the institutions of the enlarged Union will have to exercise responsibilities specifically as a consequence of the enlargement. This applies in particular to:

• Agriculture, where acceding countries have obtained the right to grant national aids for a variety of reasons (compensation for the reduction of price support, Nordic Agriculture...) subject to authorization and monitoring by the Commission.

- Fisheries, where the Commission will have to propose to the Council new management, control and technical measures to fully integrate Spain and Portugal in the Common Fisheries Policy by January 1996 - six years ahead of the date agreed in their 1985 Accession Treaty.
- Single Market legislation, where the Commission will have to propose (or adopt, in its fields of competence) new legislation on environmental, safety and health standards for a variety of products for which the new member states may maintain their own (higher) standards for a four-year transitional period.
- Transport, where the Council will have to review the special arrangements for transit of heavy vehicles through Austria ('ecopoint system') before 1998, on the basis of a report by the Commission.
- Budgetary and financial questions, in which the EP, Council and Commission will have to coordinate closely in order to adapt the Edinburgh perspectives and make the necessary quantitative adjustments. The contribution of the new Members States to the EDF will be defined in the context of the mid-term review of the Lomé Convention in 1995.

The main problem areas

The fact that the negotiations were conducted with four relatively rich EFTA countries which had, since 1977, accepted the principle of the free movement of industrial goods and had accepted much of the liberalisation of trade, services and the right of establishment and Community rules in the context of the EEA, meant that the objectives to be achieved during the enlargement negotiations did not appear to be excessively difficult in the majority of cases. Moreover, and in contrast to previous accessions, it is necessary to emphasise that these enlargement negotiations had to respect the principle of the Single Market, namely that all border controls should be abolished as from the date of accession. That obliged new approaches towards agricultural and non-tariff barriers.

Many technical and political problems have been settled in the context of the accession negotiations. Without the intention of being exhaustive, the following can be mentioned:

Customs Union and external relations

As members of EFTA, all the applicant countries already enjoyed free trade with the EU in industrial products and some processed agricultural products, but in view of accession they agreed to adapt their own customs tariffs to the Common Customs Tariff level and to accept the common commercial policy, abandoning their existing bilateral agreements and their membership of EFTA. The Nordic countries will maintain their free-trade arrangements with the Baltic Republics in the expectation of a future EU-Baltics free-trade agreement. Furthermore, the new members will be able to benefit from horizontal measures for inward, and outward, processing and tariff suspensions.

Environmental, health and safety standards

All four candidates submitted requests for derogations in order to maintain their higher national standards, a different conservation status for certain animal and plant species and related matters. Different solutions have been considered, in order to reconcile these desires for as long as EU-standards have not reached the same level, with the need to maintain the free circulation of goods. The 'third option alternative' allows the new members to maintain their present stricter rules during a period of four years. During which time the EU Directives in question will be reviewed in accordance with normal Union procedure. These reviews will be without prejudice to the outcome and will be binding on all Member States. Other solutions foresee short transitional periods, EU financing for monitoring, and technical adaptations in lists of protected animals, addition of indigenous drinks to the list of EU alcoholic beverages, etc.

Agricultural policy and regional policy

Unlike previous enlargements, this one took place within the framework of the Single Market which excludes the possibility of border controls as from the date of accession. That approach necessitated direct price alignment without the introduction compensatory amounts for a transitional period, as was done for previous accessions. With the exception of Sweden, which applies market prices for farm products which are equivalent to, or lower than, those established in the Community, the candidates have higher levels of prices and protection for their agricultural products and the 'Four' hoped/expected to maintain their farmers in the 'comfort' to which they had become accustomed.   This situation, and the difficult growing conditions of Nordic agriculture, made it necessary to link support for farmers with regional and structural questions.   For a transitional period, digressive national aids to farmers should be authorised and every candidate should receive an agro-budgetary package as a EU contribution to the cost of such aids.   At the same time, the Accession Conference agreed to create a new Objective 6 for regions with populations less than eight inhabitants/sq.km.   Full application of existing regional measures, mountain and less-favoured areas and agro-environmental measures have also been designed to avoid a decline in farmers' incomes after the alignment of agricultural prices to the lower EU levels.   National, long-term aids for specific areas will also be authorised to facilitate the integration of Nordic agriculture and small Austrian farms into the CAP.   In addition, difficult discussions took place over the fixing of milk, sugar and reference quantities and areas for some common marketing organizations.   And a system of protection for sensitive products from the agricultural and the food processing industries has been agreed.

State Monopolies

Another area in which the situation of the 'Four' is in conflict with the *acquis* and which stirs up - in some cases - strong emotions, is that of the restrictions on the production, import, export, wholesale and retail of alcoholic beverages (the four applicants) and tobacco (Austria).   During the negotiations, some of the applicants declared that their monopolies were based on important health and social policy considerations and that anti-drink groups would oppose any increased access to alcohol.   In the end, the negotiations were not too difficult, due to the fact that the adaptation of these monopolies were examined in the light of EU rules which the candidates had already accepted for the purposes of the EEA agreement.

Fiscality

Applicant countries will apply the Union's Value Added Tax system, but with some of the derogations which certain Member States currently enjoy or which are necessary to facilitate a gradual entry into the Union's taxation system. During a transitional period, Scandinavian applicants can maintain their own limits on the quantities of cigarettes and tobacco that travellers are allowed to bring, tax-free, with them. The application of these exceptions must not have any effect on the Union's own resources system for the budget, and compensation must be paid in accordance with the present budgetary regulations. The same compensation principle applies to the exclusion of the Finnish Åland Islands from the territorial applications of the EU provisions in the field of indirect taxation.

Fisheries

The negotiation of this chapter was particularly difficult in the case of Norway and was the last point to be agreed. Discussions covered access to waters, access to resources, management of resources and market access for fish. The access to waters for Finland, Sweden and Norway had been covered by an arrangement comprising principles and methods equivalent to those established in the Act of Accession for Spain and Portugal, with some adjustments of a technical nature. In access to resources, the setting of total allowed catches (TACs) and quotas reflected the fishing patterns and the EEA quotas already established. Finland and Sweden are allowed to continue traditional herring fishing for purposes other than human consumption for a transitional period, subject to scientific evidence on the evolution of the fish stocks.

Budgetary provisions

The applicant countries will pay their full contributions to the EU and ECSC budgets and to the EDF created by the Lomé Convention and will be fully involved in the EIB. Even if the budgetary forecasts are very difficult - as witnessed in previous accessions - the first estimates of the Commission showed that the four new Members will contribute 6.000 million additional ECU per annum to the EU budget while they will receive some 4.500 million ECU from it. According to these estimates, only Finland will receive more than its contribution to the Union's budget. However, in addition to payments under the different Community policies, it was agreed that the new members will receive financial compensation over the first four years (1995-98) to take account of problems related to the inevitable time-lag involved in the implementation of the CAP and as an equivalent of the commitments made under the EEA Agreement (financial cohesion mechanism and the financing of the flanking policies). The total agro-budgetary package offered by the Union to the Four amounted to 3596m ECU over the period 1995 - 98: 1255 for Sweden, 971 for Austria, 855 for Finland and 515 for Norway.

Other specific questions

Aside from these general questions, there were several other issues either of interest to just one of the applicants or having special political and economic importance for only some of them.   Among these can be mentioned:

- Road transit agreement requested by Austria in order to maintain the right to restrict the transalpine transit of heavy vehicles through Austria and bilaterally to and from Austria (already covered by the 1992 Transit Agreement lasting to 2004).   It was only the solution of this question in the final round of negotiations on 1 March 1994 which permitted the Union and Austria to conclude the negotiations.
- Protocols on the special rights for the Sami people in Sweden, Finland and Norway.
- The Åland Islands are to benefit from special arrangements (approved by 73.7 per cent of the Ålanders in a separate referendum held on 20 November 1994).
- Finnish insurance companies will be obliged to separate their pension schemes from other insurance activities, and the market will be open to companies from other countries.
- The new members are being granted a five-year adaptation period before applying in full the right of foreigners to acquire secondary residences on their soil.
- Because of its geographical position and the exclusion of sea transport from the European networks project, Finland obtained a declaration stating that due attention must be paid to Finnish sea transport in the relevant Union initiatives.

The Maastricht 'non-issues'

At the beginning of the negotiations, there was some concern about the full acceptance by the new applicants of the EU *acquis* on EMS and the future EMU (chapter 23), on CFSP (chapter 24), on Justice and Home Affairs Policy (chapter 25) and on other provisions of the Maastricht Treaty (chapter 26).   However, all the acceding countries have accepted the present primary and secondary legislation on these matters in full without debate.   Nevertheless, this does not prejudge the position they will take vis-à-vis potential future developments in the EU concerning these issues.   The question of neutrality is specially relevant in this context.

The institutional debate

Even if all the outstanding questions with the Four were solved during the March 1994 talks, the deadline of 1 January 1995 established at the Copenhagen European Council was always uncertain until the last moment. One of the elements of this uncertainty is particularly relevant to the thinking on the future of the EU: the institutional one.   This has never been a problem between the EU and the applicants, but a problem among the Twelve when the UK and Spain initially wanted to change the proportion of weighted votes in the Council of Ministers needed to block EU decisions.   The wish of these two countries to keep the blocking minority at 23 votes, instead of raising it to 27 (the latter being the mathematically correct figure resulting from the global number of votes going up from 56 to 70), has met with the opposition both of other EU members and of the EP.

In spite of the pressure put upon them, the UK and Spain - fearing a dilution of their power in the case of the former and a weakening of the Mediterranean front in the case of the latter - publicly resisted increasing the threshold from 23 to 27 until a final compromise was reached during several Council meetings and only agreed *in extremis* at the meeting held in Ionnina on 29 March 1994.   The Ionnina Compromise is not part of the Act of Accession, neither is it attached to the minutes of the Conference, according to which the question of the weighting of votes and the threshold of the qualified majority is to be examined during the 1996 IGC.   This setback clearly confirmed that the institutional debate demanded by the EP and several EU members, just before the Copenhagen Summit of

June 1993, was totally necessary before attempting the first EU enlargement and the future prospect of an EU of 20 or 25 members.

The EP also expressed concern on these issues in its resolutions of 11 February 1993, subsequent to the Hänsch Report of 17 November 1993 on institutional reforms and the CFSP and of 9 February, 1994 on the state of the enlargement negotiations with Austria, Sweden, Finland and Norway. At the last stage of the Conference, the EP recalled, prior to giving its positive assents on enlargement, the need for institutional reforms and a deepening of the EU; while the Council, in March 1994, invited all European institutions to establish a report on the functioning of the TEU and decided to create - in the European Council in Corfu (June 1994) - a 'Reflection Group' to prepare institutional options for the future in view of the 1996 IGC.

Along these lines Mr Theodoros Pangolos, the Greek Foreign Affairs Minister who chaired the last sessions of the 14-month accession negotiations with the Four said:

> Now that this is done, now that I have done my duty ... I honestly want to say that this decision was wrong ... the EU should not have undertaken new responsibilities before the Community structure deepens, before we proceed to necessary structural and economic changes, before we satisfy the preconditions set by the Maastricht Treaty.

The impact of the 1995 enlargement

The EU and the three new member countries are natural partners sharing a common heritage in terms of tradition and history. They also have a common commitment to pluralistic democracy and a market economy open to the world. The Three have reached a high standard of living and an advanced system of social protection.

The first consequence of the enlargement was the increase in size of the EU from 12 to 15. It adds 788.000 sq.kms and 22 million inhabitants. In terms of Gross Domestic Product, the gain is 7 per cent, and in terms of per capita income the former average of 15.840 ECU will reach 15.951 due to the higher level of the newcomers (even after the decline in transactions with ex COMECON countries) vis à vis the EU-12 average. Therefore, the impact of this enlargement in terms of market size should not be exaggerated. Secondly, most of the trade creation and trade diversion effects associated with accession have already taken place, or are taking place, as a result of the implementation of the EEA which virtually removed all barriers among the '12' and the former-EFTA countries. In terms of international position and political weight, Finland and Austria are bringing new geographical borders and links with Russia and eastern Europe, and these two countries along with Sweden are bringing clear leadership in international institutions and bodies contributing positively to a post-cold war geopolitical dimension for the EU.   Meanwhile, the quantitative institutional approach followed in this enlargement has lead to a simple mechanical adaptation of official languages (from 9 to 11), of the total number of components of the EU institutions, and a proportional increase in the capital of EIB.

As far as the question of voting rights in the Council is concerned, the qualified majority is fixed at 62 out of a total of 87 votes (4 for Austria and Sweden and 3 for Finland).   However, in accordance with the Ionnina compromise, 'if members of the Council representing a total of 23 to 25 votes indicate their intention to oppose the adoption of a decision by a qualified majority, the Council will do everything in its power to reach a satisfactory solution that could be adopted by at least 65 votes'.

A new issue is the distinction now made between large and small Member States for the purpose of ensuring that there is always at least one large Member State in the Troika when the enlarged Council establishes the new rotation order for the Presidency in the Council.

In spite of these relatively limited effects, the 1995 Nordic and Alpine members are expected to put pressure on the EU and to bring leadership to the Community in social standards, environmental matters, openings to Third World countries, welfare state requirements, democratic controls by both the EP and national Parliaments, and other questions that will help the Union to deepen at the same time that it expands after the 1996 IGC.

Bibliography

Andriessen, F. (1991), *Towards a Community of twenty-four?*, speech delivered at the 69th Assembly of Eurochambers, Brussels, 19 April 1991.

Avery, G. (1992), *Enlargement: the Major Challenge for the Nineties*, address delivered at the Top Forum Europe, organized by the European Movement on 5 March 1992.

Avery, G. (1994), 'The European Union's Enlargement Negotiations', *The Oxford International Review*, vol. V, no. 3, Summer 1994, pp. 27-32.

Baldwin, R. et al (1992), *Is Bigger better?: The Economics of EC Enlargement*, Centre for Economic Policy Research (Monitoring European Integration No. 3), London.

Baldwin, R. (1992), On the importance of joining the EC's Single Market: The Perspective EFTA Members, *Rivista Di Politica Economica*, Anno 82, no. 12, pp. 267-84.

Balkir, C. and Williams, A.M. (eds) (1993), Turkey and Europe, Pinter, London.

Boos, D. and Forman, J. (1995), Enlargement: Legal and Procedural Aspects, *Common Market Law Review*, no. 32, pp. 95-130.

Commission Of The European Communities (1992), Europe and the Challenge of Enlargement, *Bulletin Of The European Communities*, Supplement 3/92.

Commission Of The European Communities (1992), The Challenge of Enlargement: Commission Opinion on Austria's application for membership, *Bulletin Of The European Communities*, Supplement 4/92.

Commission Of The European Communities (1992), The Challenge of Enlargement: Commission Opinion on Sweden's application for membership, *Bulletin Of The European Communities*, Supplement 5/92.

Commission Of The European Communities (1992), The Challenge of Enlargement: Commission Opinion on Finland's application for membership, *Bulletin Of The European Communities*, Supplement 6/92.

Commission Of The European Communities (1993), The Challenge of Enlargement: Commission Opinion on Norway's application for membership, *Bulletin Of The European Communities*, Supplement 2/93.

Council Of The European Communities (1992), *European Council in Lisbon 26-27 June 1992: Conclusions of the Presidency*, Doc. S1 (92) 500.

Council Of The European Communities (1992), *European Council in Edinburgh 11-12 December 1992: Conclusions of the Presidency*, Doc. S1 (92) 1050.

Council Of The European Communities (1993), *European Council in Copenhagen 21-22 June 1993: Conclusions of the Presidency*, Doc. SN 180/93.

Council Of The European Communities (1993), *European Council in Brussels, 10 - 11 December 1993: Conclusions of the Presidency*.

Council Of The European Communities (1994), *Report on the results of the negotiations on the accession of Austria, Sweden, Finland and Norway to the European Union*, drawn-up under the responsibility of the Presidency of the Council in cooperation with the Commission services, Doc. SN 1838/2/94 REV.2, 9 March 1994.

Denton, G. (1993), *Federalism and European Union after Maastricht*, **Wilton Park Papers**, no. 67.

Ems, E. (1992), The economic impact of the EEA, *Integracio Europea*, no. 12, pp. 44-54.

European Parliament (1993), Resolution on the Structure and Strategy for the European Union with regard to its enlargement and the creation of a Europe-wide order, Resolution A3-0189/92 adopted on 20 January 1993, *Official Journal Of The European Communities*, vol. 36, no. C 42, 15 February 1993, pp. 124-30.

Gazzo, E. (1994), Enlargement and Council voting: national interests and common interests, *Agence Europe*, 22 and 23 March 1994, editorials.

Granell, F. (1986), 'Les périodes transitoires des différents élargissements de la Communauté Européenne', *Revue Du Marché Commun*, no. 294, pp. 95-100.

Granell, F. (1988), 'Spain and the Enlargement of the EC', in Greilsammer, I. and Weiler, J.H.H. (eds): *Europe and Israel: Troubled Neighbours*, Walter de Gruyter, Berlin, for the European University Institute, Florence.

Granell, F. (1990), 'La cuarta ampliación de la Comunidad Europea', *Politica Exterior*, vol. IV, no. 17, pp. 175-86.

Granell, F. (1994), 'Les conditions d'adhésion de l'Autriche, la Finlande, la Norvège et la Suède à l'Union Européenne', *Revue Du Marché Commun*, Novembre, pp 583-591.

Granell, F. (1994), *EFTA and the enlargements - past, present and future - of the European Union*, Paper presented to the Seminar on the Accession Negotiations held at the Sussex University European Institute, 29 and 30 September.

Granell, F. (1995), 'The European Union's Enlargement Negotiations with Austria, Finland, Norway and Sweden', *Journal Of Common Market Studies*, vol. 33, no. 1, March 1995, pp. 117-41.

Hopkinson, N. (1993), *Widening the European Community after the Edinburgh Summit*, Wilton Park Papers, no. 64.

Hopkinson, N. (1994), *Enlarging the European Union in Northern, Central and Eastern Europe*, Wilton Park Papers, no. 81.

Jorna, M. (1995), 'The Accession Negotiations with Austria, Sweden, Finland and Norway: A Guided Tour', *European Law Review*, vol. 20, no. 2, April 1995, pp. 131-158.

Lansing, P. and Bye, P.J. (1992), 'New Membership and the Future of the EC', *World Competition Law And Economics Review*, vol. 15, no. 3, pp. 59-73.

Maillet, P. et al (1992), 'La demande d'adhésion de la Suède', Special Number of *Revue Du Marché Commun*, no. 59, pp. 449-555.

Marin, M. (1993), El horizonte de la ampliación, speech delivered at the Maastricht Conference organized by EUROFORUM, 4 February 1993, in *El Escorial*.

Marin, M. (1994), *Presente y Futuro de la Unión Europea*, speech delivered at the Circulo de Economía, Barcelona, on 10 March 1994.

Michalski, A. and Wallace, H. (1992), *The European Community: The Challenge of Enlargement*, London, Royal Institute of International Affairs (European Programme Special Paper).

Murphy, A. (1993), *The European Union and the Challenge of Enlargement*, Dublin, Irish Council of the European Movement.

Nicholson, F. and East, R. (1987), *From the Six to the Twelve: The Enlargement of the European Communities*, Longman, Essex.

Nugent, N. (1992), 'The deepening and widening of the EC: Recent evolution, Maastricht and Beyond', *Journal Of Common Market Studies*, vol. 30, no. 3, pp. 311-28.

Office For Official Publications Of The European Communities, Documents concerning the Accession of the Republic of Austria, the Kingdom of Sweden, the Republic of Finland and the Kingdom of Norway to the European Union, *Official Journal Of The European Communities*, special issue, no. C241, 29 August 1994, and No. L1 of 1 January 1995 (for updating after the Norway non-accession). Also No. C1 of 1 January 1995 for the revised Ionnina Institutional Gentleman Agreement.

Pedersen, Th. (1988), *The Wider Western Europe: EC Policy Towards the EFTA Countries*, Royal Institute of International Affairs, Discussion Paper no. 10, London.

Pedersen, Th. (1994), *European Union and the EFTA Countries: Enlargement and Integration*, Pinter, London.

Redmond, J. (ed) (1994), *Prospective Europeans: New Members for the European Union*, Harvester Wheatsheaf, London.

Reisch, G. (1993), *The Future of EFTA-West and East*, speech by the Secretary-General of EFTA in Helsinki, 29 November 1993.

Sardelis, CH. (1993), EC Enlargement and the EFTA Countries, *Economic Papers Of The EC Commission*, no. 100.

Smidt, St. (1994), 'The Power of Greater Europe', *European Brief*, vol. 1, no. 6, July/August, pp. 50-1.

Subedi, S.P. (1993), 'Neutrality in a Changing World: European Neutral States and the EC', *International And Comparative Law Quarterly*, vol. 42, no. 2, pp. 238-68.

Tovias, A. (1995), *The impact of the EEA Agreement and the Last Enlargement on Israel's Economy: Alternative Policy Responses*, Centre for European Policy Studies Working Document no. 94.

Van Den Broek, H. and Granell, F. (1994), La futura ampliación de la Unión Europea, *Informacion Comercial Espanola*, no. 728, April, pp. 67-74.

Vdyrynen, R. (1993), Finland and the EC: Changing Elite Bargains, *Cooperation And Conflict*, vol. 28, no. 1, pp. 31-46.

Wallace, W. (1990), *The Transformation of Western Europe*, Chatham House Papers, (London, Pinder for the Royal Institute of International Affairs.

Westendorp, C. (1992), *Profundizar y ampliar la CE*, in Los retos del 93, Madrid: Secretaria de Estado para las Comunidades Europeas, pp. 13-24.

Yatanagas, X. (1982), 'Problems of Greece's Accession to the EEC', *Journal Of Common Market Studies*, June, pp. 333-59.

Note

1.   A part of this paper is a revised text of the article 'The EU's Enlargement Negotiations with Austria, Finland, Norway and Sweden', published in the *Journal of Common Market Studies*, vol. 33, no. 1, March 1995, pp. 117- 41.

4 Austria, Transit and the Environment

DAVID PHINNEMORE

Austria's referendum on membership of the European Union (EU) in June 1994 resulted in a clear vote in favour of accession. This was widely welcomed both in Austria and within the EU. However, while popular and political endorsements of membership suggest that Austria will be an enthusiastic member of the EU, it is no guarantee that accommodating the Austrians in an enlarged Union will be problem-free. As in the cases of Finland and Sweden, Austria's entry into the EU brings with it new challenges for the Union. One of these is the issue of Alpine transit which, given Austrian membership, now becomes a domestic EU concern. Moreover, it requires the EU to focus more on the impact of transport on the environment. A second challenge is the issue of the environment in general. Austria, along with Finland and Sweden, is among the most environmentally-aware countries in Europe. Enlargement will thus increase pressure on the EU to raise environmental standards and pursue more environmentally-friendly policies.

The purpose of this chapter is to examine Austria's accession to the EU and reflect on the issues of Alpine transit and the environment within the context of the 1995 enlargement. The first half of the chapter provides a broad overview of how Austria became a member of the EU. Austria's position in the accession negotiations will be discussed with attention then being focused on the country's referendum and the ratification of the Accession Treaty. The second half of the chapter concentrates on the issues of transit and the environment within the context of Austria's membership of the EU and the 1995 enlargement generally. The terms of the Accession Treaty are discussed and an indication provided as to the extent to which enlargement will affect future policy developments within the Union.

Moving towards Brussels

Austria's integration policy has consistently been aimed at achieving the closest possible form of relationship with the then European Community (EC) without undermining the country's status as a neutral state.[1] Hence, up until 1989 emphasis was placed on creating a relationship short of full membership. Thus Austria participated fully in the Maudling negotiations in the late 1950s; doggedly, yet unsuccessfully, attempted to become an associate member of the EC in the 1960s; committed itself wholeheartedly to the 1972 free trade agreement with the EU; and played a prominent role in developing EU-EFTA relations in the late 1970s and the 1980s.

With the EU moving closer towards the completion of its internal market during the second half of the 1980s, however, Austria began to focus its attention more on actually becoming a full member of the Community. Changes of policy within the main political parties and the governing coalition led to the federal government submitting an application for membership in July 1989.[2] While developments in central and eastern Europe were to reduce the significance of neutrality in the context of the Austrian application, negotiations on membership were not forthcoming. Indeed, it was to take the Commission over two years to produce its opinion on the Austrian request for membership.[3] In the meantime, Austria had to content itself with negotiations towards the establishment of the European Economic Area (EEA) - an arrangement which the Austrian government from the outset consistently argued was only a means to an end. That end was membership. Only when the EEA negotiations had been completed and a final treaty signed, was the EU willing to begin formal discussions, and then negotiations, on Austrian membership.

Negotiating membership

When membership negotiations opened in February 1993, the Austrians were quick to emphasise two things.[4] Firstly, they stressed their acceptance of the *acquis* and the principles of the EU. Particular emphasis was placed on Austria's acceptance of the objectives and the development of the Common Foreign and Security Policy (CFSP). Secondly, the Austrians expressed a desire to see the negotiations concluded swiftly. However, this was not a foregone conclusion. Austria drew the EU's attention to several issues of particular interest. These would prove to be major items on the table during negotiations, particularly since they were often high on the other applicants' lists of priorities.

Firstly, Austria attached special importance to the maintenance of its high environmental standards. To this end, it sought permanent and temporary derogations in a variety of areas relating to the use, marketing, labelling and classification of dangerous substances, the protection of the ozone level, the treatment of dangerous waste, and levels of lead in petrol. Moreover, it was stressed that the EU should raise its relevant standards to the level of those applied by the Austrians. This principle was shared by the other applicants, each of which was intent on retaining its existing national standards. Sweden, Finland and Norway each placed strong emphasis on one or more of the areas highlighted by the Austrians. In addition, they wished to maintain existing restrictions on pesticides (Sweden and Norway) and the sulphur content of certain fuels (Finland).[5] Hence, on the issue of maintaining environmental standards, Austria was in good company. The chances of finding an acceptable outcome during the negotiations were thus good. Moreover, the EU was aware that the environment was a highly sensitive political issue in the applicant states and could play a significant role in the referenda.

Similarly, the EU was conscious of the sensitivity of the second issue to which the Austrians attached particularly importance - Alpine transit. Here, the Austrians made strong requests that the provisions of the 1991 agreement limiting the number of EU lorries crossing Austria and reducing exhaust emissions be maintained. As envisaged by the Commission and the Austrians, this was to be one of the core issues in the accession negotiations. Indeed, transit would be the last negotiating chapter to be closed.

Thirdly, Austria sought to maintain existing laws restricting foreign ownership of property. Such a negotiating aim reflected fears that the unrestricted acquisition of land and property, particularly in the popular Alpine region, would force up prices to the detriment of the local population and lead to a shortage of land. Similar concerns were also voiced by the other applicants. In an attempt to gain support for its position, Austria made reference to the Protocol on the acquisition of property in Denmark contained in the Treaty on European Union (TEU) which allows the Danes to maintain existing legislation on the acquisition of second homes.

The fourth item of particular concern to Austria was social policy. Here, the Austrians were intent on maintaining domestic standards and being allowed to develop domestic social and incomes policies further.

Moreover, the government wished to retain the right to take appropriate measures to safeguard the interests of the domestic labour force from the impact of the free movement of workers. Finally, there was a desire to retain the ban on women working at night.

The final issue to be highlighted was agriculture. Here, Austria expressed two concerns. Firstly, it argued that farmers in mountainous regions of the country could not be fully subjected to the rules of the Common Agricultural Policy (CAP) given that their work was indispensable for the maintenance of the Alpine environment. A special arrangement would thus have to be sought. Secondly, the Austrians resisted having to reduce overnight the high prices traditionally paid to their farmers. This would be necessary under CAP rules.

In each of the cases noted, the Austrians did win concessions, albeit in the form of derogations rather than exemptions.[6] As discussed in greater detail below, each of the applicants won the right to maintain existing environmental standards for four years after accession. Moreover, the EU undertook to revise existing environmental legislation with a view to raising standards. On the transit issue, Austria succeeded in having the main principles and objectives of the 1991 Transit Agreement transferred to the Accession Treaty. However, as discussed below, modifications to the 1991 agreement were introduced. On the issue of the foreign ownership of property, Austria, along with the other applicants, was granted the right to maintain existing legislation regarding secondary residences for five years from the date of accession. In addition, it was noted that member states could adopt non-discriminatory measures on land-use planning and environmental protection to restrict land purchases and construction.[7] With regard to social policy, it was stressed during the negotiations that responsibility for this lay with the member states. Moreover, it was stated that the role of the EU was to set minimum standards. On the areas of particular concern to the Austrians, it was noted that the EU would take appropriate measures if the free movement of workers were to have an adverse impact of the Austrian labour market.[8] Finally, the Austrian government was granted until 2001 to amend existing legislation banning night work for women in line with the EU principle of equal treatment for men and women.[9] Finally, on the question of agriculture, it was agreed that Austrian farmers generally would receive decreasing levels of compensatory payments from the EU and Austrian budgets for the next four years. Mountain farmers would be granted special subsidies from the EU's structural funds.[10]

The referendum and ratification

The terms of membership negotiated were generally welcomed in Austria since the EU had accommodated in some form most of the government's demands. What remained now was to complete the process of ratification. The focus of this was the legally-binding referendum required under Article 44 of the Austrian constitution. Prior to this taking place, however, the Accession Treaty had to be presented to Parliament. Committee discussions in the *Nationalrat* began on 18 April 1994. Once these had been concluded, both chambers voted on the necessary Federal Constitutional Law concerning EU membership. On 5 May 1994 the *Nationalrat* adopted the law by 140-35 votes.[11] Two days later the *Bundesrat* followed suit with 51 of the 62 members voting in favour.[12] In the meantime, on 4 May, the European Parliament (EP) gave its overwhelming assent to Austrian membership.[13]

With parliamentary approval for the law secured, attention switched to the referendum. The date chosen - 12 June 1994 - was significant. Early on in government deliberations, it was decided that the referendum would not take place on the same day as the elections to the National Assembly scheduled for October 1994. This would allow voters to concentrate on the issue of membership and reduce the likelihood of a protest vote against the government. This was important as results from provincial elections were showing marked dissatisfaction with the government parties. In this respect the timing of the referendum appears to have been only partially successful. Opinion pollsters after the referendum did detect evidence of a protest vote.[14] A further strategic decision was the actual choice of 12 June. Initially, late June had been favoured so as to allow more time for the necessary enabling legislation to be adopted. However, it was feared that the Euro-elections in the second week of June might result in an increase in support for the far-right within the EP, thus discouraging Austrians to support membership.[15] Hence, it was felt that the referendum should coincide with the elections to the EP. It was also argued that this could be 'politically positive', since it would draw people's attention to the democratic aspirations of the EU.[16]

The referendum - actors and issues

The 'yes' campaign was spearheaded by the government's two coalition parties, the Austrian People's Party (ÖVP) and the Social Democrats

(SPÖ). Both were forceful in their support for membership, although their campaigns differed in emphasis. The ÖVP, for example, concentrated on the enhanced security Austria would enjoy as an EU member and the increased role the country would be able to play in European developments.[17]   The SPÖ also gave prominence to the influence argument, but the party tended to place greater emphasis on the social and economic benefits of membership.[18]   Of the other political parties, support for the 'yes' campaign came from the small Liberal Forum, a new party created in February 1993 following a minor split within the Austrian Freedom Party (FPÖ).   One Green MP, Monika Langthaler, also campaigned in favour of membership. Outside of parliament, support came from industrialists and trade unionists alike,[19] and from all the major newspapers.   Also, expert assessments of the economic impact of membership tended to support the government.[20]   Such an alliance of major forces meant that the 'yes' campaign not only had at its disposal the machinery of government, but it was also well funded.   Consequently, campaign information on the benefits of membership was plentiful.

The 'no' campaign was led by the populist leader of the right-wing FPÖ, Jörg Haider, with support for a 'no' vote also coming from the majority of members of the Green Alternative party.   The two parties campaigned separately, however.   Haider's campaign for a 'no' vote was not implicitly a vote against membership.   Indeed, the FPÖ has consistently favoured membership of the EU since the 1950s.   Rather, Haider ran a populist campaign under the slogan 'Austria First', in which he advocated a renegotiation of the terms of accession.[21]   The aim of such an approach was clearly to attract popular support away from the two government parties.

The actual campaign was fought on two levels.   Firstly, there was the exchange of fairly sober arguments in favour of and against membership.   Major players here included the Foreign Minister, Alois Mock, and the Prime Minister, Franz Vranitzky.   The information campaigns of the government and the coalition parties played a significant role in this respect, although opinion polls have suggested that they were of lesser importance in influencing the outcome.[22]   At a second level, the campaign was characterised by blatant scare-mongering, particularly during the latter stages.   Both sides were equally guilty in allowing the tone of the campaign to degenerate.   On the 'no' side, Jörg Haider was particularly quick to spread scare stories of mass immigration, Mafia-styled corruption and job losses.   Among the more bizarre stories were those concerning future imports of chocolate made from blood and lice-infested yoghurt.   In responding, the government was quick to raise the spectre of currency crises, tax increases and higher unemployment if a 'yes' vote was not forthcoming.[23]

There appear to be two reasons why the campaign became dominated by scare-mongering. Firstly, much of the blame has to be placed on the tactics adopted by the FPÖ, and in particular, its leader, Jörg Haider. The second reason, and one which accounts more for the behaviour of the government parties, was the declining support for membership as indicated by opinion polls. For most of the period since the issue of membership entered the political arena in the second half of the 1980s, there had generally been more people in favour of joining the EU than against.[24] Indeed, in March 1994 when the negotiations with the EU were concluded, the 'yes' campaign had a lead of 31 percentage points.[25] However, this represented a peak in support for membership. Thereafter, the gap between the supporters and opponents narrowed considerably. Indeed, during the two weeks prior to the referendum, some polls indicated that the 'yes' campaign only had a lead of 2-3 per cent.[26] The impact of this narrowing of the gap and the fact that a 'yes' vote could not be guaranteed created a degree of panic within the government coalition. Memories of the 1978 referendum on the Zwentendorf nuclear power station did not inspire confidence. Then, the government had seen a consistently solid majority in favour of the proposed power station turn into a narrow majority against on the day of the referendum.[27] Thus complacency over a 'yes' victory was out of the question. Hence, an effort had to be made to rally support in favour of membership. Given the pressure of time, the fact that most pro-EU arguments had been exhausted over the previous years, and the need to counter the populist claims being made by the 'no' campaign, government pronouncements were naturally panic-ridden. Given the actual outcome of the referendum, the panic seems to have been unwarranted.

The referendum result

The result of the referendum was an overwhelming 'yes' to membership. In a turnout of over 81 per cent, almost two-thirds (66.58 per cent) of the votes were cast in favour of Austria acceding to the EU.[28] Thus, over 54 per cent of the electorate voted 'yes'. The extent of the margin in favour surprised commentators and campaigners alike. Moreover, the fact that all the provinces voted 'yes' as well, came as even more of a surprise. As indicated in Table 4.1 support was highest in Burgenland (74.59 per cent), the easternmost province and the province due to gain the most financially from EU structural funds. Levels of support higher than average were also recorded in Steiermark (68.69 per cent), Kärnten (68.02 per cent) and Nord-Österreich (67.80 per cent) - three provinces which, along with Burgenland, share borders with the countries of central and eastern Europe.[29] Also of note was the majority in favour of membership in the Tirol (56.42 per cent) - the province most sensitive to the environmental problems caused by EU transit traffic.

Exit polls conducted on the day of the referendum indicated that support for EU membership appeared to be greater among men (70 per cent) than among women (62 per cent).[30] They also indicated that a majority in each age group voted 'yes'. However, the percentage of younger voters (those under thirty) which voted in favour of membership was notably lower (55 per cent) than the percentage of voters over sixty (70 per cent). Generally speaking, as the age of the voter increased, so did the likelihood of a 'yes' vote. As for the voting tendencies of the various social groups, the polls suggested that farmers were the only sector in Austrian society which generally voted 'no'. Estimates of what percentage opposed membership ranged from 60 per cent to 73 per cent.[31] With regard to the social profile of the 'no' voters, these were deemed to be 'modernisation-losers', a social group characterised by poor educational background, unemployment, social and financial insecurity, and political alienation.

The list of motives for people voting 'yes', was headed by the perceived economic benefits of membership (39 per cent). In second place was the need to avoid Austrian isolation (19 per cent). Somewhat surprisingly, 17 per cent of 'yes' voters indicated a belief in European unity as a motivating factor. Other reasons cited for voting 'yes' were the general advantages of membership (17 per cent), jobs (14 per cent), and security (13 per cent). While relatively few motives appear to have been behind the 'yes' votes, exit polls indicated that a larger number of factors seem to have motivated people into voting 'no'. These range from the general disadvantages of membership (26 per cent), the problems faced by farmers (23 per cent) and concern for the environment (20 per cent) to a loss of identity (11 per cent), the import of poor quality goods (10 per cent) and hostility to foreigners (8 per cent).

Table 4.1 Results of the Austrian referendum on EU membership, 12 June 1994

	Turnout Votes	Turnout %	Yes Votes	Yes %	No Votes	No %
Burgenland	199 099	93.4	146 947	74.6	50 062	25.4
Steiermark	722 531	79.6	493 308	68.7	224 902	31.2
Kärnten	339 455	80.7	228 461	68.0	107 417	32.0
N-Österreich	999 738	89.6	670 303	67.8	318 405	32.2
Vorarlberg	175 603	79.2	115 883	66.4	58 754	33.6
Wien	810 473	71.5	529 384	65.8	274 721	34.2
O-Österreich	823 839	84.5	532 929	65.3	282 687	34.7
Salzburg	282 161	81.2	181 790	64.9	98 310	35.1
Tirol	348 402	76.5	195 483	56.4	150 970	43.6
Sub-Total	*4 705 297*	*81.3*	*3 095 260*	*66.4*	*1 556 779*	*33.6*
Postal Votes	64 155		51 484	80.3	12 671	19.8
Total	**4 769 452**		**3 145 981**	**66.6**	**1 578 850**	**33.4**

(Source: *Der Standard*, 13 June 1994; *News from Austria*, 8 July 1994.)

Completing ratification

Once the referendum was over, it was left to the Austrian parliament to complete the ratification process.[32] This was delayed, however, as a result of the country's general election in October 1994. Hence, it was not until 11 November 1994 that the *Nationalrat* successfully voted by 141-40 votes in favour of membership.[33] The instruments of ratification were then duly signed and deposited with the Italian government on 24 November 1994. Domestic ratification was thus complete. Austria now looked forward to acceding to the EU on 1 January 1995.

Accession and the transit issue

The transit issue was the most prominent and politically sensitive issue in Austria's negotiations with the Twelve.[34] By contrast, it was of no more than marginal interest to the other applicants. Had the Swiss been involved in the negotiations, then the overall importance of transit within the context of the enlargement would undoubtedly have been greatly higher. As it was, however, Austria was left alone to secure its basic aim of having the terms of the 1991 Transit Agreement included in the Act of Accession. In many respects this was achieved. Moreover, the Austrians gained a commitment to promote rail and combined transport links from the EU.

As indicated, the Austrians succeeded in the negotiations in having the main elements of the 1991 agreement, albeit at times modified, included in the Act of Accession.[35] These are as follows:

- the principle that rules relating to transit should apply to the entire territory of Austria;
- the objective of gradually reducing emissions of exhaust fumes via a 60 per cent reduction in nitrogen oxide emissions before the year 2004;
- the so-called eco-points system of quantitative restrictions on the number of transit journeys undertaken by lorries over 7.5 metric tonnes;
- the 38 metric tonne weight limit on lorries in transit through Austria.[36]

In addition, agreement was reached on certain other transport-related issues. Hence, the liberalisation of bilateral traffic between Austria and the member states of the EU is to take place on a step-by-step basis, with full liberalisation being achieved by 1 January 1997; [37] and cabotage is to be fully realised by 1 July 1998. Also, Austria is allowed to maintain its agreements on road traffic with the countries of central and eastern Europe.

While all this appears quite positive, Austria did have to make one notable concession. During the negotiations, the fixed 12-year duration of the Transit Agreement's provisions was dropped. It was replaced by the so-called '3+3+3 model' which provides for the periodical review of the attainment of the original Transit Agreement's environmental objectives - the 60 per cent reduction in nitrogen oxide emissions. The new model expires, at the latest, on 31 December 2003, a year earlier than under the original Transit Agreement. The main elements of the '3+3+3 model' are as follows:

- for the first three years of membership (i.e. until 31 December 1997), the existing provisions of the Transit Agreement will apply;
- before this first three year period has expired (i.e. probably during 1997), the Council of Ministers will meet to assess whether the environmental objectives concerning emissions have been achieved. Unless the Council decides by unanimity (i.e. with Austria's assent) that this is the case, the provisions relating to transit in the Act of Accession will remain valid for a further three years. If unanimity is reached, then the provisions will cease to apply;
- before the end of this second three year period (i.e. before 1 January 2001), a scientific study is to be carried out to assess whether the environmental objectives of the original Transit Agreement have been achieved. The focus of the study will be the envisaged 60 per cent reduction in nitrogen oxide emissions. If the study reveals that the objectives have not been achieved, the provisions relating to transit in the Act of Accession will remain valid for a further three years (i.e. until 31 December 2003). However, the Council of Ministers may, acting by a qualified majority, agree to adopt alternative measures designed to reduce harmful emissions by 60 per cent by the end of 2003. If this is the case, the provisions relating to transit in the Act of Accession will not apply after 31 December 2000.

At present, it seems likely that the current arrangement governing transit through Austria will remain in place until a least the end of 2000. In all probability, Austria will use its veto in 1997. However, whether the eco-points system will be extended for the final set of three years up until 2004 is open to question. Pressure on the Austrians to drop all restrictions on transit traffic as soon as possible will undoubtedly increase for three reasons. Firstly, the derogations granted to Austria undermine the principles of free movement central to the internal market. Consequently, all efforts will be taken to limit the time during which the restrictions will be in place. Secondly, as the volume of EU trade with the countries of central and eastern Europe increases, in particular with Hungary, Romania and Bulgaria, there will be a greater demand for transit across Austria. This will be in addition to the existing demands from Greece and Italy for greater access. Moreover, if and when stability returns to the region of the former Yugoslavia, the re-establishment of trading links will create further pressure for transit across Austria. Finally, there is the knock-on effect of Switzerland's referendum in February 1994 banning transit after 2004. If the Swiss government does place further restrictions on transit traffic through Switzerland, pressure will increase on the Austrians to reduce their restrictions.

The outcome of the negotiations on transit did involve a watering down of the provisions of the original 1991 Transit Agreement. However, the importance the Austrians attached to the transit issue provides a strong indication of how significant transport and the environment will be in the enlarged Union. Indeed, during the negotiations the Austrians succeeded in forcing the EU to acknowledge the need to deal more fully with transport issues in general in the future. Hence, the EU has committed itself to enhancing the provision of rail and combined transport; developing and utilising existing rail capacity; and including named routes in Austria in the development of trans-European networks. One result of this is that the Brenner axis high-speed train/combined transport link has been identified as a priority project for EU funding under the Trans-European Networks (TEN) plan.[38] The EU has also gone out of its way to inform the Austrians of the measures taken so far to help solve the environmental problems caused by heavy goods vehicles.[39]

As a member, it is to be expected that Austria will monitor closely the EU's fulfilment of the above commitments. Moreover, the Austrian government's White Book on European Integration Policy published in December 1994 listed several areas in which the Austrians would be pursuing action at the EU level. These included the development and competitiveness of environmentally-friendly transport systems; transport safety; the development of rail networks; and the introduction of minimum environmental and technical standards on motor vehicles in central and eastern Europe.[40] Whether Austria will be successful in achieving its objectives with regard to transport remains to be seen. Progress is, however, likely given that transport issues are often closely linked with the environment - a policy area to which all of the new members attach high priority.

Accession and the environment

As indicated above, the environment was an area on which each of the applicants placed great emphasis during the negotiations. Nevertheless, EU sensitivity to the concerns of the potential new members meant that the negotiating chapter on the environment was closed relatively early in December 1993. Hence, other than in the context of the Alpine transit issue, the environment did not feature in the closing stages of the accession negotiations.

The outcome of the negotiations for each of the applicants was generally the same.[41] Firstly, all agreed to adopt the *acquis* with regard to the environment. Somewhat surprisingly, this will actually involve a raising of standards in some cases. Austria, for example will have to adopt higher EU standards in areas such as gene technology and eco-auditing. Secondly, where environmental standards are higher than in the EU, each of the new members is permitted to maintain these standards for a period of four years after the date of accession (i.e. until 31 December 1998). Such derogations only apply to a limited number of areas. These are as follows:[42]

- classification, packaging and labelling of pesticides and other dangerous substances (A, F, S);
- marketing and use of certain chemical products (A, F, S);
- composition of fertilisers and batteries (A, F, S);
- sulphur content of gas oils (A, F);
- trade in waste (A - two year derogation only);[43]
- ban on recycling PCBs and PCTs (A, S).[44]

In addition, Austria is also allowed to maintain indefinitely its ban on leaded petrol. Moreover, concerns among the Swedes and Austrians regarding the EURATOM Treaty's reference to the promotion of nuclear energy were allayed. Sweden is allowed to continue with its phasing out of nuclear reactors by 2010, while Austria may retain its 1978 ban on the establishment of nuclear power stations. A Joint Declaration attached to the Accession Treaty states that each of the member states is to determine its own nuclear energy policy. Also, the new members are not obliged either to participate in nuclear energy projects developed within the EU or to handle nuclear waste.[45] A further joint declaration acknowledges Sweden and Finland's attachment to the Non-Proliferation Treaty.[46] While such declarations are not legally-binding, the sensitive nature of nuclear power and the limited importance attached to realising the aims of the Euratom Treaty should ensure that the positions adopted by the new members will not be undermined.

The derogations listed above are accompanied in the Accession Treaty by a commitment from the EU to reviewing existing standards with a view to raising them. This review, welcomed by the more environmentally-minded of the existing member states, is to take place during the four-year period up until the end of 1998.[47] However, there is no guarantee that the EU will have either completed the envisaged studies or raised its standards to the level of the applicants by the end of 1998.[48] Moreover, the commitment is contained in a non-binding declaration. At the end of the four year transition period, it is assumed that the entire existing *acquis* relating to the environment will apply to the new members.[49] It has been suggested, however, that Austria will seek to have the transition period extended if the review of environmental standards proves inconclusive.[50] The likelihood that such an extension will be granted is open to question. The Finns, meanwhile, have insisted that the EU member states will have to align their standards with the higher standards of the new members and not vice-versa.[51] Although the situation remains unclear, if after the transition period the EU has not raised its standards, the new member states will be able to justify the maintenance of higher national standards under Articles 36 and 100a(4) of the Treaty of Rome.

Despite this, it is generally expected that the 1995 enlargement will result in advances in the area of environmental policy. Although significant progress cannot be guaranteed, pressure for the raising of standards and for the development of greater environmental awareness will increase. Similarly, it is to be expected that the EU will be encouraged to promote environmental issues further as part of its external relations. There are several reasons for anticipating such pressures. Firstly, the EU has committed itself, in the Act of Accession, to reviewing its existing environmental legislation and policy. Given the high profile of environmental issues and the resolute stance adopted by the new members in defence of their domestic legislation, it is likely that this review will see an increase in EU standards. Secondly, enlargement will raise the number of more environmentally-conscious member states. Hence, the adoption of environmental measures is likely to be easier, particularly given the shift to qualified majority voting under the TEU. Support for current proposals on air quality, and CO_2 emissions is thus likely to receive a boost. Thirdly, the governments of the new member states have all committed themselves individually to increasing Europe-wide environmental standards by pursuing the adoption of appropriate measures at the EU level.[52] Indeed, the governments and the 'yes' campaigns generally in each of the three states argued strongly that EU membership provided the most effective means of promoting trans-national environmental regulation. In Finland and Austria, members of green parties actively campaigned for a 'yes' vote for this reason. Finally, the new members will be keen to raise the profile of environmental issues in the context of the EU's external relations, particularly with regard to the countries of central and eastern Europe. Austria has already drawn attention to the need to encourage these countries to adopt environmentally conscious energy and transport policies,[53] while Finland and Sweden are naturally concerned about pollution problems in the Baltic Sea, the Baltic States and the former

USSR.[54]

However, the impact enlargement will have on EU environmental policy may not be as great as initially anticipated, despite claims that the environment will be a priority issue for the new members. Firstly, the decision of Norway not to join the EU denies the environmental lobby of potentially its most outspoken advocate of radical policies on the environment. Secondly, the three new members wield only eleven votes out of the eighty-seven available in the Council. Their impact on voting will thus be limited. Thirdly, there are environmental issues on which the new members have differing views. Finnish and Swedish forestry and wood pulp industries, for example, remain opposed to current Commission proposals on eco-packaging and paper recycling.[55] Finally, the desire of the new members to protect their national standards could lead to further environmental nationalism and a less collective EU approach to solving environmental problems.[56]

Conclusion

The fact that almost two-thirds of those Austrians who voted in the 1994 EU referendum supported membership of the Union suggests considerable support for Austria becoming fully involved in the European integration process. However, it would be unwise to assert that the 'yes' camp's margin of victory means that the Austrians, as EU members, will be wildly enthusiastic about the Union. Long-term support is most likely to depend on whether tangible economic benefits result from membership. Moreover, it would be inadvisable to conclude that the nature of the referendum result and the commitment of the Austrian government towards the EU will make it easy for the Union to accommodate Austria as a new member. The outcome of the accession negotiations clearly indicates that there are issues about which the Austrians will be especially vocal. Two of the most prominent of these will be transit and the environment.

On transit, the dogged determination of the Austrian negotiators to retain the essential principles and elements of the 1991 agreement highlights the sensitivity of the issue in Austria. It is to be expected, therefore, that, at the various stages in the '3+3+3' model where major decisions are to be taken, Austria will remain steadfast in requiring that the proposed reductions in emissions are realised before contemplating any concessions. Despite pressure form EU members and non-members, it is unlikely that the **Austrians will be challenged** over the transit issue. Beyond the commitments it made to Austria in the Accession Treaty, the EU is likely to remain sensitive to popular opinion on transit, given the need to promote and not undermine public support for the Union's activities.

The same is true with regard to the environment, not only in Austria, but also in Finland and Sweden. Popular support for EU membership in the new member states will depend in part on the Union fulfilling its commitment to increase environmental standards. As the Austrians, Finns and Swedes have all pointed out, the environment is a priority issue for them. The impact they will have in voting terms may be small, but their forthright advocacy of environmental awareness and higher standards will not pass by unnoticed. This has already been evident in the countries' vocal opposition to France's resumption of nuclear testing in the South Pacific in 1995. Moreover, if by 1998 the EU has not brought its environmental standards in line with those of the new member states, the end of the transition period will not pass quietly.

The 1995 enlargement was originally viewed as probably the most straightforward the EU would undergo. Nevertheless, in enlarging to include Austria, Finland and Sweden, the Union has found itself faced with new challenges. Among the more prominent of these are those which relate to the sensitive issues of transit and the environment. Each of the new members has entered the EU with its own expectations, interests and priorities. The extent to which the Union responds to these will have a significant bearing on how the governments and peoples of the new members evaluate EU membership.

Notes

1. For details of Austria's relations with the EC prior to membership, see Breuss, F. and Stankovsky, J., *Österreich und der EG-Binnenmarkt*, Signum-Verlag, Wien, 1988; Esterbauer, F. and Hinterleitner, R. (eds), *Die Europäische Gemeinschaft und Österreich*, Wilhelm Braumüller, Wien; Gehler, M. and Steininger, R. (eds), *Österreich und die europäische Integration*, Böhlau, Wien 1993; Koch, K, 'Austria: The Logic of Accession', in Redmond, J., *Prospective Europeans: New Members for the European Union*, Harvester Wheatsheaf, Hemel Hempstead, 1994, pp. 40-58; Luif, P., *Neutrale in die EG?: Die westeuropäische Integration und die neutralen Staaten*, Wilhelm Braumüller, Wien, 1988; Luif, P., 'Austria', in Wallace, H. (ed), *The Wider Western Europe: Reshaping the EC/EFTA Relationship*, RIIA/Pinter, London, 1991, pp. 124-45; Schneider, H., *Austria and the EC*, RIIA Discussion Paper 24, London; Wieser, T. and Kitzmantel, E., 'Austria and the European Community', *Journal of Common Market Studies*, vol. 28, no. 4, pp. 431-49.

2.   See Rack, R., 'The Austrian Application', in Church, C.H. (ed), *Widening the Community Circle*, UACES Occasional Paper no. 6, London, 1990, pp. 31-41; Pedersen, T., *European Union and the EFTA Countries - Enlargement and Integration*, Pinter, London, 1994, pp. 79-85.

3.   EC Commission, 'The challenge of enlargement - Commission opinion on Austria's application for membership', *Bulletin of the European Communities*, Supplement 4/92, 1992.

4.   Mock, A., *Erklärung anläßlich der Eröffnung der Beitrittsverhandlungen mit der Europäischen Gemeinschaft am 1*, Februar, Bundeskanzleramt, Wien, 1993. For more details of the Austrian negotiating position see: Bundeskanzleramt/Bundesministerium für Auswärtige Angelegenheiten (1993), *Vortrag an den Ministerrat: Europäische Gemeinschaft; Aufnahme der Beitrittsverhandlungen; grundsätzliche österreichische Verhandlungsposition; Verhandlungsvollmacht*, Bundeskanzleramt, Wien, 21 Jänner 1993.

5.   For further details, see Bjørnvig, B. (Rapporteur), *Report of the Committee on the Environment, Public Health and Consumer Protection on the environmental aspects of the enlargement of the Community to include Sweden, Austria, Finland and Norway*, European Parliament Session Document A3-0008/94, 1994.

6.   The Treaty of Accession is reproduced in OJC 241, 29 August 1994. For a discussion of the negotiations and details of the outcome, see Rack, R. and Renner-Loquenz, B., 'Die Beitrittsverhandlungen Österreichs mit der EU', *Österreichisches Jahrbuch für Internationale Politik 1993*, Böhlau, Wien, 1994, pp. 116-145; Bundeskanzleramt (1994a), *Bericht der Bundesregierung über das Ergebnis der Verhandlungen über den Beitritt Österreichs zur Europäischen Union (Fassung 6. April 1994)*, Bundeskanzleramt, Wien; Kubitschek, M. et al. (1994a), 'Verhandlungsergebnisse mit der Europäische Union (Zusammenfassung)', *AW Spezial*, no. 70, pp. 1-5; Kubitschek, M. et al. (1994b), 'Verhandlungsergebnisse mit der Europäische Union', *AW Spezial*, no. 71, pp. 1-7; Jorna, M. (1995), 'The Accession Negotiations with Austria, Sweden, Finland and Norway: A Guided Tour', *European Law Review*, vol. 20, no. 2, pp. 131-158.

7.   Articles 70, 87 and 114 of the Act of Accession, *Joint Declaration on secondary residences*.

8.   *Joint Declaration on the free movement of workers*.

9.   Kubitschek et al. (1994a), p. 5.

10.   See Mannert, J., 'Bauern - EU - Zukunftsängste', *Freie Argumente*, vol. 21, no. 5, 1994, pp. 51-53.

11.   Support for the law came from the SPÖ, the ÖVP, the Liberal Forum, and one Green MP. Only members of the FPÖ and the Greens voted against.

12. One SPÖ delegate, Martin Wabl, joined opponents of the law and voted against his own government.

13. The EP voted by 374 to 24 votes with 61 abstentions - a wide margin but a slightly narrower one than those for Finland, Norway and Sweden.

14. 'EU-Nein der Modernisierungs-Verlierer', *Der Standard*, 14 June 1994.

15. 'Outsiders hit by a strain of Euro-fever', *Financial Times*, 3 June 1994.

16. *Agence Europe*, 1 April 1994, p. 4.

17. See Busek, E., *Europa-Erklärung der ÖVP*, ÖVP, Wien, 1994; 'Wir sind Europäer. Österreicher bleiben wir - Europa-Kongreß der Österreichischen Volkspartei', *Pressedienst der ÖVP-Bundespartei*, Wien, 15 Mai; 'Appell des ÖVP-Präsidiums zur Volksabstimmung', *ÖVP-Pressedienst*, 9 June.

18. See SPÖ, *Warum wir für Europa sind*, SPÖ Bundesgeschäftsstelle, Wien, 1994; SPÖ, *Ja zu Österreich - Ja zu Europa: Erklärung des Bundesparteirates der SPÖ über den Beitritt Österreichs zur Europäischen Union*, SPÖ Bundesgeschäftsstelle, Wien, 1994.

19. See, for example, Vereinigung Österreichischer Industrieller, *Wir Stimmen für Europa*, Vereinigung Österreichischer Industrieller, Wien, 1994.

20. See Breuss, F. et al., 'Effekte eines EU-Beitritts für die Gesamtwirtschaft und für die einzelnen Sektoren', *WIFO Monatsberichte*, 1994, pp. 18-33. The report estimated that membership could lead to a real increase in GDP of 2.8 per cent by the year 2000, create 42,000 new jobs, and see consumer prices drop by 3.25 per cent. See also the rather inconclusive report Kramer, H., 'Austria and the European Union', *WIFO Monatsberichte*, 1994, pp. 12-17 and the author's comments in 'Austria torn by EU referendum', *The Guardian*, 1 June 1994.

21. See Haider, J., *Unser Weg nach Europa*, FPÖ Bundesgeschäftsstelle, Wien, 1993; Haider, J., *Nein heißt Ja zu Neuverhandlungen*, FPÖ Bundesgeschäftsstelle, Wien, 1994.

22. In one opinion poll, the government's campaign was cited by 23 per cent of people as a factor contributing to a 'yes' vote. The other factors were Alois Mock (57 per cent), the media (42 per cent), Franz Vranitzky (27 per cent), Erhard Busek (7 per cent), the church (5 per cent), Brigitte Ederer (3 per cent). See 'Sieg der Sternsinger?', *Profil*, 20 June 1994. A second opinion poll indicated that only 25 per cent of the electorate used the government's campaign material as a source of information. The main sources of information cited in the poll were TV/radio (79 per cent), newspapers (71 per cent), private discussions (52 per cent), workplace discussions (25 per cent). See 'Werbekampagne nicht entscheidend', *Die Furche*, no. 24, 1994.

23.   See 'Austrians get the Euro hard-sell', *The Guardian*, 13 March 1994; 'Austria torn by EU referendum', *The Guardian*, 1 June 1994; 'Austrians in a fever over EU referendum', *Financial Times*, 8 June 1994; 'Knives are out as Austrians prepare to vote on Europe', *The Guardian*, 9 June 1994; 'Tyrolean die-hards lead No campaign', *The Guardian*, 11 June 1994; 'Austrians put faith in EU', *Financial Times*, 13 June 1994.

24.   See, for example, Luif (1991), pp. 136-138. The gap was narrowing, however, in 1992/93, such that some opinion polls showed greater support for a 'no' vote. See Pedersen (1994), pp. 84-85.

25.   *Agence Europe*, 5 March 1994. For subsequent poll findings, each of which showed a decrease in support for membership, see *Agence Europe*, 1 April 1994; *Agence Europe*, 16 April 1994.

26.   'Outsiders hit by a strain of Euro-fever', *Financial Times*, 3 June 1994; 'Austrians in a fever over EU referendum', *Financial Times*, 8 June 1994.

27.   Lenhardt, D., '1994 - Austria's "super election year"', *Austria Today*, 1/94, 1994, pp. 4-7.

28.   Of the 4,705,297 voting slips completed, 43,258 (0.92 per cent) were deemed to be invalid.

29.   According to official sources all administrative 2373 districts in Austria voted in favour of membership. The highest 'yes' vote recorded was 86.47 per cent in Mattersburg in the Burgenland. The highest vote against membership was in the village of Kaisers in the Tyrol (88.64 per cent). See *News from Austria*, 24 June 1994, p.3. See also 'Die Ergebnisse in den Städten', *Die Presse*, 13 June 1994.

30.   The poll findings cited come from a telephone exit poll conducted by Fessel and GIK on the day of the referendum, as cited in 'EU-Nein der Modernisierungs-Verlierer', *Der Standard*, 14 June 1994.

31.   However, doubts were cast on these figures by the Farmers Federation, which pointed out that even in Nord-Österreich, the major agricultural province in the country, 68 per cent of voters voted 'yes'.

32.   In the meantime the Constitutional Court dismissed a case contesting the validity of the referendum result. See *Agence Europe*, 2 September 1994, p. 3; *News From Austria*, 16 September 1994, p. 3.

33.   *News from Austria*, 25 November 1994, p. 3. Owing to the poor showing of the ÖVP and SPÖ in the general election on 9 October 1994, the government coalition had to rely on the ten votes of the Liberal Forum in order to gain the required two-thirds majority for the necessary constitutional amendment. The Green Alternatives also voted in favour. There were two abstentions.

34. For details of the negotiations on the transit issue, see the following editions of *Agence Europe*: 13 March 1993, p. 7; 23 September 1993, p. 10; 30 September 1993, p. 8; 11 December 1993, p. 6; 02 March 1994, p. 6; 03 March 1994, p. 6; 04 March 1994, p. 6. See also Seidl-Hohenveldern, I., 'L'Union européenne et le transit de marchandises par rail et par route à travers l'Autriche', *Revue du Marché commun et de l'Union européenne*, no. 389, 1995, pp. 320-387. The 1991 Transit Agreement is reproduced in OJL 373, 22 December 1992.

35. See Act of Accession, Protocol no. 9 on road, rail and combined transport in Austria. See also Bundeskanzleramt (1994a), pp. 15-17; Kubitschek et al. (1994a), p. 4; Puwein, W., 'EU-Verkehrspolitik: Mehr Wettbewerb durch Deregulierung', *WIFO-Monatsbericht*, 1994, pp. 90-91; *Agence Europe*, 4 March 1994, p. 6.

36. Austria is, however, to phase out its right to impose fines on lorries breaching the 5 per cent tonnage excess allowed. See Joint Declaration on weights and dimensions for road transport vehicles.

37. The Austrians also committed themselves to introducing by 1 January 1997 an electronic control system to speed up the monitoring of transit traffic as part of the eco-points system and to prevent claims for two bilateral journeys being made in order to avoid transit restrictions.

38. The Corfu Summit also identified the Ørensund fixed link between Denmark and Sweden as a high priority TEN project. See EC Commission, *European Council at Corfu 24-25 June 1994 - Presidency Conclusions*, EC Commission, London, 1994, Annex 1; 'New network plans gather speed', *Financial Times Exporter*, 5 October 1994. See also Joint Declaration on the Brenner base tunnel. In the week preceding the referendum in Austria it was announced that provisional agreement on the Brenner base tunnel had been reached. In December 1994, the European Council at its Essen Summit, added the Nordic Triangle rail/road project involving Sweden and Finland to the list of priority TEN projects. See EC Commission, *European Council Meeting on 9 and 10 December 1994 in Essen - Presidency Conclusions*, EC Commission, London, 1994, Annex 1.

39. Declaration on the solution of the environmental problems caused by traffic of heavy goods vehicles.

40. Bundeskanzleramt, *Weißbuch der Bundesregierung*, Bundeskanzleramt, Wien, 1994, pp. 16-21 and 70-73. See also 'Österreichs Weißbuch im Herbst', *Die Presse*, 23 June 1994; 'Transit: Unser Ziel ist erreicht', *Freie Fahrt*, 4/94, April 1994.

41. See Bundeskanzleramt (1994a), pp. 6-10; Bundeskanzleramt (1994b), *Umwelt - Die Ergebnisse der Beitrittsverhandlungen mit der EU*, Bundeskanzleramt, Wien; Köppl, A. et al., 'Umweltpaket und umweltpolitischer Gestaltungsspielraum', *WIFO Monatsberichte*, 1994, pp. 97-99. For details of the negotiations on the environment issue, see the following editions of *Agence Europe*: 14 May 1993, p. 5; 11 June 1993, pp. 7-8; 17 July 1993, pp. 9-10; 20-21 December 1993, p. 6; 22 December 1993, pp. 7-8; 23 December 1993, p. 6.

42.   See Articles 69, 84 and 112, and Annexes VIII, X and XII of the Act of Accession. See also EC Commission, *The Enlargement of the European Union*, Background Report ISEC/B19/94, London, October 1994.

43.   In a Joint Declaration on the shipment of radioactive waste, issued by the Twelve and Finland, it is confirmed that no member state is obliged to accept specific shipments of radioactive waste.

44.   Pending the adoption of EC legislation banning the recycling of PCB and PCT, the new members may maintain their bans. See Joint Declaration: Norway, Austria, Sweden: on PCB/PCT.

45.   See Joint Declaration on the application of the Euratom Treaty.

46.   See the Joint Declarations on the Non-Proliferation Treaty.

47.   See also Joint Declaration on standards for the protection of the environment, health and products safety, and Joint Declaration on Articles 32, 69, 84 and 112 of the Act of Accession.

48.   *Agence Europe*, 23 December 1993, p. 6.

49.   See Joint Declaration on standards for the protection of the environment, health and product safety.

50.   Bundeskanzleramt (1994a), pp. 7-8; Köppl et al. (1994), p. 98; *Agence Europe*, 23 December 1993, p. 6. See also Kubitschek et al. (1994a), pp. 4-5. The declaration the Austrians alluded to does not, however, appear in the version of the Accession Treaty contained in OJC 241, 29 August 1994.

51.   *Agence Europe*, 22 December 1993, p. 8.

52.   See the speeches of Gro Harlem Brundtland, Thomas Klestil, Martti Ahtisaari, and Carl Bildt at the signing of the Treaty of Accession, reprinted in *Council of the European Union Press Release 7979/94*, Corfu, 24 June 1994. For Austria, see also the wide-ranging proposals drawn up by the Austrian government in Bundeskanzleramt (1994c), pp. 55-74.

53.   'Khol: Mit Beitritt zur EU beginnt neue aussenpolitische Ära', *ÖVP Pressedienst*, 27 July 1994.

54.   'Positive role for a bigger club', *Financial Times*, 15 November 1994.

55.   'Heading south - A Survey of the Nordic Countries', *The Economist*, 5 November 1994, pp. 4-5, 17; 'Industry shrugs off krona rise', *Financial Times*, 15 November 1994, p. 3.

56. Barnes, P.M., 'The Impact of Finland and Sweden on European Union Environmental Policy', in Lovenduski, J. and Stanyer, J. (eds), *Contemporary Political Studies*, Political Studies Association, Belfast, 1995, pp. 1188-1194.

5 Sweden and Security

LEE MILES

Introduction

For the neutral states of Austria, Finland and Sweden, security questions were central to their respective positions regarding the European Union (EU).[1] To some extent, these countries faced similar strategic limitations and albeit to a limited degree, responded to these challenges in the same manner.[2] In contrast, the other applicant involved in the 1995 accession round - Norway, did not have a major problem with security when it came to accession to the EU.[3]

For almost thirty years, all three countries shared the same strategic objections regarding EU membership and security concerns provided one of the main official reasons for why Austria, Finland and Sweden did not apply for full EU membership. In each of the three cases, full EU membership was constantly rejected on the basis that it was incompatible with their neutrality policies. In addition, these neutral applicants also faced the same dynamic challenge presented by the changes which have engulfed eastern Europe since 1989 and introduced a new set of variables into their strategic thinking.

By 1989, the major strategic obstacles to EU membership were virtually removed and all three eventually responded to this by submitting full membership applications. Austria was the first to realise the implications of eastern Europe's transformation, submitting her application even as the changes were taking place in 1989. Sweden and Finland took longer to reconcile their traditional security concerns with EU membership but went on to lodge full membership applications in July 1991 (Sweden) and March 1992 (Finland). Ultimately, all three EFTA neutrals accepted the Common Foreign and Security Policy (CFSP) embodied in the Treaty of European Union (TEU).

This chapter will encompass four aspects. First, it will assess to what extent security questions were instrumental in determining the EFTA neutrals' relationship with the emerging EU. In particular, Swedish-EU

86

relations and the concept of Waite's 'Swedish Paradox' will be used as the primary model for analysis, although comparisons will be made with the strategic concerns of Austria and Finland. Secondly, it will analyze the importance of security issues as part of the enlargement negotiations and comment upon Sweden's EU accession terms. Thirdly, the chapter will focus on Sweden's transition to EU membership and provide a brief evaluation of the Swedish referendum on full membership (13 November 1994) in order to assess whether security questions were central to the Swedish EU debate. Finally, it will consider Swedish (and to a lesser extent, Austrian and Finnish) perspectives regarding the future development of the CFSP.

Defining and comparing neutrality - Swedish, Finnish and Austrian experiences

To some extent, Austria, Finland and Sweden have been viewed by external observers as a common grouping (along perhaps with Switzerland) as these countries each hold the dual title of being EFTA members and neutral states. According to Jessop and Deák, the modern idea of international neutrality revolves around the two central concepts of non-participation in a state of war between two other states and at least, some degree of impartiality or equal treatment of belligerents.[4] However, the onset of the Cold War and the creation of a nuclear Europe meant that this neutrality definition was politically adapted to be the complete non-participation in international conflicts.[5]

At face value then, Austria, Finland and Sweden share common perspectives regarding European security and are adherents to what Hakovirta calls 'European neutrality'. In other words, each of these countries was confronted with the dilemma of being an 'asymmetrical' neutral. On the one hand, these countries are advanced industrialised countries sharing Western values of liberal democracy and a market economy and thus, in political and economic terms, have closer links with the West. Yet, on the other, their neutrality policies required that they remained officially detached from the bloc division of Cold War Europe and thus avoided at all costs, being drawn into any future European wars.

Nevertheless, there were always noticeable differences between all three countries concerning the nature of their neutrality. In many ways, the type of neutrality policy that each country followed was dependent on two main variables. First, their geographical location and consequently, the country's strategic importance to the geopolitics of the European continent and more correctly, to the interests of the two superpowers at this time.[6] This, in practice, decisively influenced whether their neutrality could be deemed to be 'active' or 'passive'. For example, Finland's geographic position as a neighbour of the Soviet Union meant that superpower interest in its behaviour was much greater than in say that of Sweden (which does not share a 1,300 kilometre long border with a superpower) and ultimately ensured that Finland's neutrality policy was passive.

Secondly, the legal status of their neutrality and in particular, whether the respective countries' neutrality is recognised by other countries (and especially the two superpowers of the USA and USSR) in international law. It could be argued that this correlates to the difference between 'permanent' neutrality under international law, which formally commits a state to neutrality in all wars by international treaty (and obliges it to avoid such peacetime ties that would make its neutrality in war impossible or unlikely) and 'continuous and conventional' neutrality under which countries tend to call their policies neutral, but do not enjoy the relative safety that their neutrality is recognised by others under international law.

In reality then, the neutrality of these countries could also be divided into 'voluntary' or 'mandatory' categories, even if at times, neutral countries do behave in similar ways regardless of the category. The differences may actually just be variations in emphasis. None the less, there is usually a direct relationship between the voluntary/mandatory and the passive/active categories. For example, the voluntary nature of Swedish neutrality has meant that the country consistently tried to maintain its neutral status through an active role in international affairs.

Yet, as Hakovirta argues, for any neutrality policy to be effective and successful, the policy must also have credibility and enjoy respectability.[7] Neutrality policy must be consistently and clearly espoused and foreign policy decisions must be compatible with the country's declared neutrality in order that in practice, the neutral states' actions are predictable and that the neutral state can 'pre-empt international calculations on its position'.[8] In essence, neutrality incorporates 'a never ending determination to build confidence - both at home and abroad- in its chosen position'[9] and usually also compels neutral countries to maintain strong defence forces; thereby convincing other states of their resolve to remain neutral. Yet, to some extent, Austrian, Finnish and Swedish neutrality also required that the external environmental 'norms' were also stable. Their neutrality policies were 'crystallised' by the bloc-division of Europe that seemed, until 1989, to be relatively solid. In one sense, their neutrality was more credible as they focused upon being detached from specific bloc arrangements that divided Europe.

In the Swedish case, neutrality was, in effect, voluntary and active. For Sweden, neutrality is a relatively old and deep-seated concept, originating from 1814 and lasting, in its most advanced form, up until around 1990-91. Swedish foreign policy was defined narrowly as 'non-alignment in peace time in order to retain neutrality in the event of war'. The key problem for the Swedes was always that, unlike postwar Austria and Finland, their neutrality was not recognised in any international treaty and that in practice, Sweden's neutrality was voluntarily maintained by her own singular effort.

Thus, Hakovirta's concerns over neutrality being credible and predictable were emphasised in Swedish policy making. Policy incorporated a number of features that helped to ensure neutrality's durability. In the first place, the concept of Swedish neutrality enjoyed considerable domestic political and public support and a consensus existed amongst Swedish political parties regarding security policy until around 1990-91. Swedish neutrality was viewed domestically as highly successful and as having managed to ensure that the country remained aloof of any European wars for over a century. This feature is, of course, not unique to Sweden, as both Austria and Finland also enjoyed a high degree of domestic consensus on the merits of neutrality. However, Sweden officially pursued an 'unflinching' policy of neutrality (*orubbligt*) under which, according to official doctrine, the credibility of Swedish neutrality required complete public support.[10]

Secondly, Swedish neutrality policy was deemed to include both domestic and international aspects[11] and influenced all areas of Swedish decision-making. For Sweden, the continued credibility of her neutrality was paramount and consequently, every major foreign and domestic policy decision taken by her governments needed to be compatible with the parameters of neutrality policy. In effect, there existed 'an unusual domestic politics of independence' within Sweden. Her governments followed a dual strategy of, on the one hand, frequently reiterating her non-alignment in the international arena and on the other, trying to ensure that internal as well as foreign policies took account of, and sought to reinforce, Sweden's neutrality.

Hence, Sweden's economic and international trade policies were influenced by her security policy and her neutrality. Economic sovereignty was not to be fundamentally compromised. Participation in supranational economic organisations, such as the EU or indeed any military alliance, was regarded as incompatible with the independence requirements of a credible neutrality policy. Sweden, for a long time, could only flirt with the idea of European Community (EC) membership, and even then principally on its own terms. When the EU was created in 1958, Sweden resisted membership. She objected on the basis of the EU's supranational organisational features, the responsibilities that Sweden would have to undertake as part of the EU's customs union, and more specifically, the EU's Common Commercial Policy (CCP) which empowered the EU to conclude commercial agreements with non-member states (Article III, Treaty of Rome).[12] Sweden also remained deeply suspicious of any EU overtures aimed at achieving monetary integration, (such as the Werner Plan), as these were perceived as undermining her economic, as well as political, sovereignty and consequently, her policy of neutrality.

Thirdly, the credibility of Swedish neutrality also required a strong attachment to 'Total Defence' and the maintenance of large armed forces, with supporting technological and military industries, to reinforce the country's independence from foreign powers. In practice, this was translated into high defence spending per capita and the development of a large domestic armaments industry. Sweden's defence expenditure was consistently one of the highest in western Europe and her forces were disproportionately large compared to the size of her population. For example, it devoted around three per cent of its GNP to defence in the 1970s, although this steadily declined throughout the 1980s, and supplied some 70 per cent of defence requirements from domestic sources.[13] By maintaining a strong defence, Sweden's neutrality would therefore be seen to be 'active'.

In addition, Swedish neutrality was also combined with internationalism. Successive Swedish governments argued that Sweden's active role in international politics reinforced the credibility of its neutrality policy and that the linkage between the two was 'not just compatible or complimentary but mutually supportive'.[14] Sweden remains, for example, heavily involved in United Nations (UN) operations and has especially contributed to UN peace-keeping activities. For instance, Swedish troops were deployed as part of UN commands in Macedonia in 1993 and Bosnia in 1994,[15] with some 1,300 Swedish peace-keepers serving in the former Yugoslavia in 1995.[16] At times, Sweden was also fervent in displaying her 'active neutrality' by vehemently criticising the respective superpowers. For instance, in the early 1970s, Sweden heavily criticised the USA for her interventionist role in Vietnam, and during the early 1980s, diplomatic relations with the USSR were strained over alleged violations of Swedish territorial waters by Soviet submarines.

Thus, the last two aspects of a large military capability and a strong international role especially illustrate the 'active' aspects of Swedish neutrality and differentiate Swedish neutrality from that of the Austrians and the Finns. Indeed, neither Austria or Finland sought to maintain, comparatively speaking, such large forces or overseas roles as both aspects could be viewed as undermining the respective states' more delicate political and legal neutral positions.

Austria's geographic position 'at the very crossroads of East and West'[17] ensured that her neutrality was to become permanent, mandatory and in many ways passive. When Austria finally regained full sovereignty after allied occupation in the State Treaty of 1955, the country also attained the internationally recognised status of permanent neutrality, which was fully endorsed by both superpowers and blocs. Hence, Austrian neutrality was 'a mathematical function' of the East-West power conflict in which only the permanent Austrian neutrality would be acceptable to both blocs in Cold War Europe.[18] The maintenance of large armed forces, total defence and a very active international role was thus not such a viable option for Austria. Yet, despite the restrictions of permanent neutrality, the Austrians, comparatively speaking, still enjoyed rather more freedom of manoeuvre in international affairs than Finland. Austria was still able to economically integrate with the West and was a founder member of both the OEEC and EFTA.

For Finland, her neutrality was clearly the most passive of all three countries dealt with here. Policy was governed by her close proximity to the Soviet Union and the historical legacy of having fought and lost two comparatively recent wars against the Soviets in 1939-40 and 1941-1944. Finnish neutrality was essential to ensure the maintenance of the state itself and Finnish independence was only guaranteed by relatively strict adherence to the articles of the 1948 Treaty of Friendship, Cooperation and Mutual Assistance with the USSR. The 1948 Treaty (which incidently lasted until its replacement with a more limited free trade agreement in 1992) obliged Finland to remain neutral and to come to the USSR's aid if attacked by a neighbouring state.

Thus, for Finland, military-strategic issues were paramount and the maintenance of the existing and relatively peaceful status quo in Europe was the ultimate objective of Finnish foreign policy. Hence, Finnish neutrality was 'semi-mandatory' in the sense that it was fully and legally recognised by the eastern superpower and bloc, although not formally by the West. In contrast to Sweden, Finland's neutrality was completely passive and ruled out any institutional obligations that could be viewed as undermining the 1948 Treaty and antagonising the USSR. Two episodes in Finnish history - the 'Night Frost' of 1958-59 and the 'Note Crisis' of 1961-62 illustrated the sensitivity of the Soviets towards Finnish independence. Therefore, Finnish policy aimed at establishing special and limited trade arrangements with the West (such as, the 1961 FINEFTA arrangement which gave Finland associate membership of EFTA), which also indirectly took account of Soviet concerns and guaranteed the USSR certain rights. Indeed, Finland refrained from becoming a full member of EFTA until 1986, and even then only consented to this after receiving Soviet approval.

To sum up then, Finnish neutral status was the more passive, with Sweden's neutrality being the most active and Austria somewhere in between. This of course, was directly related to the respective countries' geographic position and the international status of their neutrality, with Austria's being mandatory and internationally recognised, Finland's being 'semi-mandatory' and partially recognised and Sweden's being entirely voluntary. The differing nature of Swedish neutrality was also implicit in its policy towards the EU and it is this question that the next section will address.

Swedish - EU policy - economic and political considerations

However, translating the relatively clear concept of Sweden's neutrality into practice became increasingly problematic once she began to grapple with challenge of an emerging EU during the early 1970s. Waite, for example, has argued that Sweden suffered from a 'paradox' regarding her relations with the EU.[19] Sweden has been forced to constantly seek closer trading relations with the EU in order to ensure competitive access to EU markets. The open nature of Sweden's export orientated economy, the growing internationalisation of Swedish business and the fact that from 1973, two of Sweden's largest trading partners, (the UK and Denmark) were now EU members meant that Swedish dependence on EU markets was ever growing. By the early 1970s, the enlarged EU accounted for more than 50 per cent of Sweden's foreign trade. For economic reasons then, Sweden needed at the very least, to secure preferential trading with the expanding EU and even full EU membership was increasingly attractive.

However, at the same time, the political considerations of maintaining the principles of independence and 'active neutrality' were inhibiting. They acted as obstacles to full membership, even though Sweden intermittently revised her European policy and even reconsidered EU membership. However, she maintained that full membership would have to be compatible with her policy of neutrality. Thus, from the early 1960s until 1990-91, Swedish attention focused upon the question of how to become an EU member without having to meet the complete obligations of full membership.

Sweden's first attempts at squaring this circle can be traced back to 1961. In response to Britain's announcement in July that it would apply for EU membership, Sweden proceeded in December to apply for associate Community membership as a means of strengthening its relationship with the EU. Again in July 1967, Sweden proposed opening negotiations with the Community on a flexible kind of membership after the British lodged a second application. In line with existing Swedish policy, both attempts were conditional upon any membership deal being compatible with Sweden's neutrality policy. On each occasion, the door was closed on these options when France's President de Gaulle vetoed the respective British application.

Nevertheless, by the early 1970s, two developments led to a further reappraisal of the Swedish position vis-à-vis the EU. Sweden's economy and particularly, her sensitive engineering, steels and electronics industries had become firmly integrated into EU markets. Secondly, the chances of the EU enlarging to include the UK and Denmark were now very real since the election of a more sympathetic President Pompidou in France. In August 1970, Sweden and the Community opened negotiations with the aim of establishing 'extensive, close and durable relations in a form compatible with the continued pursuit of Swedish neutrality'.[20] In the same year, Sweden also proposed a customs union between itself and the EU, allowing for fuller economic integration, while still maintaining the premise of avoiding political integration. However, the EU's adoption of the Davignon (political integration) and Werner (EMU) plans killed these initiatives as these were perceived as threatening the credibility of Swedish neutrality.

By 1971, Sweden had tried most options and had failed to provide an effective method of reconciling any form of EU membership with her neutrality. However, although these initiatives ended in failure, they did indirectly lead to clarification of Swedish policy towards the EU, which was to become the main tenet of Swedish foreign policy up until 1990. In its policy declaration on the 10 November 1970, her government formally clarified its position on the EU further by stating that Sweden 'cannot participate in such forms of cooperation on foreign policy, economic, monetary and other matters which, in our judgement would jeopardise our possibilities to pursue a firm policy of neutrality'. On 18 March 1971, the government finally announced that it had therefore come to the 'conclusion that membership is not a realistic possibility so far as Sweden is concerned' although it would continue to 'seek to attain close, comprehensive and durable economic relationships with the Communities'.[21]

In response, the *Riksdag* passed a virtually unanimous parliamentary resolution removing the issue of membership from the political agenda on the grounds of incompatibility with neutrality. This, for the most part, remained government policy until 1990. *De facto* integration was intensified while formal political integration was avoided.[22] Partly as a result of these initiatives, Sweden signed a free-trade agreement (FTA) with the EU on 22 July 1972. This agreement secured Swedish access to EU markets, without diluting neutrality and thus, formally divorced economic and political considerations. There were however, deficiencies within the FTA and the two dimensions were not completely reconciled as for example, the agreement still maintained some restrictions on specialist Swedish steel exports.

However, by the 1980s, there had been a noticeable shift in Swedish governmental attitudes. In practice, the economic attractiveness of closer relations with the EU was to eventually outweigh the political constraints of maintaining Swedish neutrality, while at the same time and in any case, the distinction (as made by Waite) between economic and political considerations was becoming blurred. Four factors were significant in revising these narrow and artificial divisions in Swedish governmental attitudes regarding the EU.

First, the growing size and rising profile of the EU was compromising Sweden's political sovereignty and its freedom of manoeuvre on foreign and trade policy matters. By the time the free trade area between the EU and Sweden was completed in 1984, the FTA was already too limited to protect Sweden's national interests. By the mid-1980s, the EU had expanded from nine to twelve members and was also about to embark on the Single European Market (SEM) programme, which was perceived as posing a threat to Swedish exports unless further access to EU markets could be secured.[23] The EU's research and development programmes, such as ESPRIT, were also attractive to Swedish business. Furthermore, the European Commission's declared intention to establish a comprehensive social policy, (as later embodied in the 1989 Social Charter) also lessened

Swedish concerns over the impact of EU membership on its generous welfare provisions.

It was not surprising then when Sweden welcomed the 1984 'Luxembourg process' and actively promoted closer EFTA-EU cooperation (especially as it did not compromise Swedish neutrality). Yet, the level of cooperation was still too limited and the concept was soon overwhelmed by the significance of the EU's SEM programme. Increasingly, the economic necessity of securing access to EU markets was overriding the political need of maintaining neutrality. Sweden's concerns regarding the EU were highlighted in a key policy paper given by the Swedish government to the *Riksdag* in 1987,[24] which directly recognised the threat of discrimination against Swedish firms if excluded from the emerging SEM and even went as far as proposing future Swedish EU membership, provided her neutrality requirement could also be reconciled.

From 1987, Sweden was officially 'shadowing' the SEM's development. Her government introduced legislation aimed at assimilating Swedish conditions with those of the SEM, providing a clear indication that economic sovereignty and political independence were being affected. Later, Sweden welcomed the introduction of the more advanced European Economic Area (EEA) concept in 1989, despite it including the creation of a supranational competition authority.

For Sweden then, the EEA was important for two reasons. First, and initially the EEA seemed to be an ideal arrangement for securing access to the SEM, without significantly compromising Swedish neutrality. Secondly, the slowness of the negotiations (especially during the 1990 Swedish EFTA Presidency) and growing Swedish frustration with its limitations were instrumental in leading to the later July 1991 application. Sweden, along with the other EFTA countries, failed to gain a sufficiently influential decision-making role in the EU's formulation of SEM legislation, even though each EFTAn would be required to accept some 12,000 pages of the EU's *acquis*. Ultimately, the failure of the EEA to fully accommodate Swedish interests in what seemed to be the best deal that could be negotiated as a non-member state finally convinced the Swedish government in 1990 that full EU membership was the only viable future option for guaranteeing her future national interests.

Nevertheless, the alterations in Swedish views were also facilitated, initially, by deeper questioning of the merits of Swedish neutrality during the 1980s and ultimately later, by complimentary changes to the strategic environment in Europe. During the 1980s, two new security problems confronted Sweden and led, albeit to limited extent, to further strategic questioning as to the continued relevance of Swedish neutrality. The first was the heightened potential threat of being dragged into war because of the growing strategic significance of the European 'High North'.[25] Ever since the 1960s, Swedish military planning had been based on a 'marginality thesis' whereby Sweden's forces only needed to be sufficiently strong enough to deter a conventional attack as both superpowers viewed the Nordic region as an area of low tension and of marginal strategic importance. However, the rapid build-up of Soviet naval forces in the Kola peninsula and its transformation into the most heavily armed territory in the world simultaneously raised the strategic importance of the Nordic area and reduced the probability that Sweden would be able to remain neutral or marginal to any ensuing conflict.

The second threat was the real problem posed by the continuing military violations of Swedish territorial waters and airspace.[26]   Reports of unidentified foreign submarines, some most likely armed with nuclear weapons, became more frequent and brazen after 1980, challenging the external credibility of Swedish neutrality.   In particular, the so-called 'Whiskey on the Rocks' episode in 1981, (when a Soviet 'Whiskey' class submarine ran aground near the Karlskrona naval base) and the even more serious Hårsfjärden intruder incident in 1982, raised doubts regarding Sweden's ability to maintain its territorial integrity (as part of 'Total Defence' strategies) and whether her 'armed neutrality' was credible in the eyes of the blocs in Europe. Thus, by the 1980s, Swedish neutrality was itself facing new strategic challenges.

However, crucially, it was the 1989 revolutions in eastern Europe that allowed for Swedish neutrality itself to be revised and defined more flexibly and with this, the last final and official obstacle to future EU membership was eliminated.   In essence, the rationales for Swedish neutrality itself had declined as Europe and its bloc arrangement was revised. Although the economic considerations were increasingly perceived as more important than the political ones, it was the strategic changes that enabled the main neutrality objections to EU membership to be virtually removed.   EU membership was, from 1989-90, increasingly compatible with Sweden's changing security policy and could now be legitimised on strategic as well as on economic grounds.

By 1990, the Social Democrat government had shifted in favour of EU membership as the only practical way of securing Sweden's economic and political interests.   At the opening of the Swedish Parliament (*Riksdag)* on 2 October 1990, Prime Minister Ingvar Carlsson outlined his vision of a developing Europe that would not be divided into blocs and argued that, under this scenario, EU membership would be compatible with Swedish neutrality.   Shortly afterwards, on 26 October 1990, the government suddenly announced that Swedish EU membership was now in the national interest and that the government would be preparing to submit an application.   This shock announcement was made as a 'footnote' to an economic austerity package which gave the impression that this was a somewhat hasty decision.   The reality was that this was the culmination of a much longer process.[27]

In December 1990, the *Riksdag* formally approved the decision to seek EU membership with 90 per cent supporting the motion, although the passed motion did also include a reference to the retention of neutrality. The December parliamentary statement sparked a small debate amongst the domestic political elites over the future of neutrality policy with highly respected officials, such as ambassador Sverker Åstrom calling for a public review.   Even so, by the 14 June 1991 (when Ingvar Carlsson gave a formal statement to the *Riksdag*), the Prime Minister was able to formally declare that Swedish membership of the EU was now 'compatible with the requirement of our policy of neutrality'.[28]

The policy revision was rationalised on several grounds.   First, that there had been important strategic changes in Europe, allowing for greater flexibility.   Secondly, the unanimity requirement for taking decisions would be maintained in any future EU foreign policy endeavour.   Therefore, the Swedish government was confident that it could avoid any commitments which would compromise its revised security policy.   Interestingly, and unlike the previous 1989 Austrian application, the Swedish full membership application did not include a reference to neutrality, although the June 1991 declaration would be difficult to ignore.[29]

However, with the formation of the Bildt non-socialist government in October 1991, there was an even more dramatic alteration to Swedish security policy.   Carl Bildt had long been an advocate of EU membership. As early as 1987, Bildt had called for a stronger European identity and an active role in European cooperation for Sweden.   In his first ministerial speech to the *Riksdag* (4 October 1991), he introduced a revised 'foreign and security policy with a European identity' and neutrality was now formally, and for the first time in one hundred years, dropped from the official rationales of security policy.   Yet, although security policy had been reduced to merely an explicit reference to 'non-participation in military alliances', the pivotal role of the Centre Party within the non-socialist coalition meant that this commitment had to be maintained as the party remained in favour of Swedish non-alignment.

Nevertheless, since 1991, the general Swedish party consensus on security policy has showed signs of cracking and is now far from 'unflinching'. Bildt's revised policy, for example, received considerable criticism from the Social Democrats, who accused Bildt of being premature in removing Swedish neutrality before it was certain that the changes in Europe were permanent.

The European Commission recognised these revisions in its August 1992 Opinion on the Swedish application and directly stipulated that her security policy had favourably evolved.[30]   This more assertive and pro-Western foreign policy was further consolidated, when Bildt claimed in 1993 that Sweden could hardly remain neutral, as defined in international law, if Russia attacked the Baltic states.[31]   His government adopted an active policy with regard to Estonia, Latvia and Lithuania and in effect, gave these three countries implicit military guarantees for their defence.

Hence, two themes are evident from this chronological study of Swedish security policy.   First, that the political and economic considerations of Swedish EU policy (as developed by Waite) became difficult to separate during the 1980s and ultimately, economic motives dominated as political sovereignty was in practice being affected by new arrangements, such as the EEA.   Secondly and more importantly, the external changes in the strategic environment accelerated this trend and formally removed the obstacle of Swedish neutrality from the question of EU membership.   The revolutions in eastern Europe provided both an opportunity and a rationale for a more narrowly defined Swedish security policy as neutrality had become irrelevant anyway, allowing for Swedish security policy to be reduced to a simple commitment to 'non-participation in military alliances' by 1993.

Sweden and the accession negotiations

Despite the European Commission's initial welcoming of the changes in Swedish policy, there still remained some scepticism about Sweden's position (along with the other two EFTA neutrals) as regards the embryonic CFSP.   All three EFTA neutrals were quick to state they were willing to accept both the *acquis* and the *finalité politique* of the TEU.

Nevertheless, in both the Commission's report, 'Europe and the Challenge of Enlargement', which was approved by the June 1992 Lisbon European Council Summit and the Commission's opinion on the Swedish application, it was specifically recognised that Sweden's participation in the definition and implementation of the CFSP (Article J.1-10, TEU) would be sensitive. All three Commission opinions on the Swedish, Austrian and Finnish applications identified their neutrality as being of 'particular concern' and that 'specific and binding assurances' would be sought from these states regarding the compatibility of their neutrality with the CFSP.

The Swedish government responded to these statements in February 1993 by stating that it was prepared 'to participate fully' in the CFSP, although her policy of non participation in military alliances remained unchanged. In other words, Sweden was not prepared to join a military alliance, but would not hamper the development of the EU by preventing other EU members from creating a common defence either. To some extent, the Swedish position partly reflected the need to simultaneously maintain a limited national consensus in Sweden and at the same time, not risk irritating her negotiating partners during the accession negotiations.[32]

This problem was reflected not only in Sweden's position on the CFSP, but also in other major areas prioritised by her government, which became the main issues for Sweden during the negotiations. These included, for example, Sweden's position on her environmental standards and that these standards were not to be compromised by EU membership and that the EU would continue its policies of 'sustainable development'. Ulf Dinkelspiel, the Minister for European Affairs, even claimed at the start of the opening of the negotiations that 'the highest level of ambition will apply in the environmental area and thus there will be no lowering of standards'.[33] In reality though, Sweden did not gain a guarantee that its high standards would not have to be lowered as a result of EU membership. Under the 'third option' agreement, it only secured a four year transitional period on environmental standards, during which a 'consultation period' would be enacted to harmonise environmental legislation.[34]

In addition, the Swedish government also perceived the EU's developing social dimension as a 'crucial corollary to economic integration'.[35] Sweden believed her collective agreements would be adequate for the implementation of directives and looked forward to the development of further rules under the TEU's social chapter. In one sense, the Swedish government's strategy was defensive in that it wanted to ensure that Sweden's advanced policies would not be compromised by EU membership. However, the most contentious issue during the negotiations was the securing of a derogation for the Swedish moist 'snus' (wet tobacco) trade which was prohibited on health grounds by an EU directive. For all these issues, the government tried to take a stern line for domestic consumption as in many ways, these were the most symbolic, cultural issues capable of losing votes for Swedish EU membership.

As regards regional policy and agriculture, the issue of Structural Fund allocation and agricultural support was less problematical for the Swedes than in the Finnish case, as Swedish agricultural reforms in 1990 and 1991 had removed many of the difficulties for her government associated with the CAP. Agricultural subsidies were comparable to CAP levels (on average only 20 per cent higher) and any reductions in agricultural subsidies from the day of Swedish accession would be less severe (compared for example, than with price reductions in Finland). However, Sweden also wanted to ensure that the allocation of EU structural funds and agricultural support would take account of her geographical location, her sparse population and her severe climate. More than a third of the Swedish population, for example, lives in areas with a population density of less than 12 inhabitants per square km (compared to the EU average of 150 per square km). She actively promoted, with the other Nordics, the case of Arctic and sub-Arctic agriculture, a 'Northern approach' to regional and agricultural policy and new criteria based on low population density in order to maintain rural populations in the North. For the most part, Sweden was satisfied with the inclusion of the new Objective 6 criteria based on low density of population agreed in the negotiations for Structural Fund allocations.

However, three issues were championed by the Swedish government - namely, the retention of the country's alcohol monopolies, the size of its budgetary contributions and greater transparency in EU decision-making. Under the EEA agreement, the Swedish government had (like Finland) accepted the EU's treaty provisions on commercial monopolies, yet the maintenance of her alcohol monopolies on health and social policy grounds was more contentious. Sweden insisted that these arrangements were a strategic part of controlling the consumption of alcohol amongst its population. The EU was supportive, especially as the future of the alcohol monopolies would also be a sensitive issue for voters during the later referendum. Hence, the accession deal was a political compromise. It provided for the abolition of the state monopolies on the import, production and distribution of alcohol, but allowed for the monopolies on retail sales to be retained.[36]

It was generally expected that Sweden would also be a substantial net contributor to the EU budget, but the issue for the Swedes concerned the size of its contribution. The severe recession in Sweden between 1990-93 forced her government to resist any excessive financial demands from the

EU, arguing, with some justification, that any large financial contribution to the EU budget would severely damage any progress aimed at dealing with the deterioration of central government finances since 1990.[37] Consequently, this was the last issue to be solved (March 1993). Indeed, both Sweden and Finland were accused by certain member states of being obstructive and of achieving 'highway robbery', regardless of the fact that this would be a sensitive issue for the Nordic governments in their future referenda. In practice though, Sweden achieved a good result in the negotiations on its budgetary contribution, gaining a budgetary rebate worth up to ECU 2 billion in the first three years as a farm adjustment payment. In fact, Sweden will only contribute a net ECU 50 million to the EU budget in its first year of membership.

In addition, the Swedish government consistently pushed the issue of greater transparency and public accountability in EU and especially, Council decision-making. Sweden welcomed the EU's movement towards more open deliberations, such as the decision to televise Council proceedings at the Birmingham Summit. Yet, the Swedes also insisted that further initiatives would need to be taken. This is partly related to Sweden's long-standing traditions of open government.[38] Sweden championed this issue comparatively more than her Nordic counterparts, despite their declared commitments to the same cause. Dinkelspiel, for example, at the start of the accession negotiations, specifically noted that open government (*offenlighetsprincipen*), free public access to official records and the protection of those giving information to the media (*meddelarfriheten*) were fundamental principles laid down in the Swedish constitution and that, 'these form an inalienable part of our political and cultural heritage'.[39]

Again, the Swedish government's prioritising of this issue reflected the domestic debate in Sweden, particularly as anti-EU forces had identified the issue of preserving Swedish democracy as being of critical significance in their campaigns against full membership. However, despite 'transparency' representing a pre-emptive strike by the Swedish government, it failed to prise any significant concessions from the EU during the negotiations. None the less, it has made progress since becoming a member and in March 1994, the Danish, Finnish and Swedish governments jointly proposed the publication of the Council's deliberations and voting outcomes.[40] In general though, Sweden gained a generous accession package, which took account of most of her concerns. The EU remained unusually flexible and considerate of the domestic problems that the

Swedish government faced in gaining public approval for EU membership on 13 November 1994. It is to this aspect that this chapter will now turn.

Evaluating the Swedish referendum on EU membership

The legacy of the September 1994 General Election

The referendum was preceded by a general election in Sweden and this formed the backdrop against which the referendum was fought. This was influential in three ways. First, there was a general consensus amongst the major Swedish political parties that this was to be an election fought solely on domestic issues. In fact, the election was fought on the issues of the Swedish budgetary deficit, levels of national debt and the problem of rising unemployment. In particular, by the time of the election, the national debt stood at SEK 1,300 billion, only slightly short of Sweden's entire GDP for 1993 of SEK 1,450 billion.[41]   Thus, in practice, the issue of EU membership, and even the future shape of Swedish security concerns, was divorced from the election and left for debate in the future referendum.

Secondly, the Social Democratic Party won a resounding victory and turned in its best performance since 1982, capturing 45.3 per cent of the votes and 161 of the 349 parliamentary seats. Ingvar Carlsson returned as Sweden's prime minister leading a minority administration. This result had major implications as regards the EU debate. The return of a Social Democratic administration, for example, actually increased the chances of a positive vote in the later referendum. This seemed somewhat ironic given that the Social Democratic party remained split on the issue and that the previous Bildt government had been enthusiastically in favour of full membership. It was argued that given the fact that the Social Democrats were split on the EU issue, there was a greater chance of a 'Yes' vote with a Carlsson government. Dissident Social Democrats would be less inclined to vote negatively in the referendum and against a Social Democratic government, than if a non-socialist administration had led Sweden into the referendum campaign.

This was also partly the reason why Carlsson cited the EU issue as one of the reasons for refusing to consider a coalition with the pro-EU Liberal Party after the election. He claimed that a coalition with the Liberals could have triggered strong negative reactions among the trade union movement and among active party workers. It was suggested that only a Social Democratic government could guarantee a majority of voters in favour of

EU membership, especially once Ingvar Carlsson had pledged to campaign for EU membership after the Social Democratic party conference in June 1994 approved this policy by 2-1.

A Social Democratic government would also slow the Bildt government's shift from a policy of neutrality. Carlsson, after all, had previously criticised Bildt for his foreign policy statements concerning Sweden's role in the Baltic region. However, in the Social Democratic government's first foreign policy declaration in 1994, Carlsson maintained that the security and development of the Baltic states was important to Sweden and cooperation would be intensified.[42]

Thirdly, those parties who opposed EU membership did well in the elections and those parties identified as being pro-EU generally suffered. The pro-EU Liberal Party saw its share of the vote drop from 9.1 per cent (1991 general election) to 7.2 per cent (1994). In contrast, the anti-EU Greens and the Left Party increased their share of the vote from 3.4 per cent (1991) to 4.5 per cent and from 4.5 per cent (1991) to 6.2 per cent respectively. The election increased the number of anti-EU members of Parliament from around 20 to between 60-65. Aside from the Greens and the Left Party, seventeen Social Democrats were also in the anti-EU camp. This partly explains why two well known EU opponents were included in the Social Democratic Cabinet (Margareta Winberg as Minister for Agriculture and Marita Ulvskog as Minister for the Interior).

The referendum campaign

The legacy of the 1994 general election created an unusual situation for the party campaigners. On the one hand, the central role of the Social Democrats seemed to be confirmed. Yet, the divisions within the Social Democratic Party (in which it was estimated that up to 45 per cent of supporters were anti-EU) and the appointment of prominent anti-EU campaigners to the new Social Democratic Cabinet meant that Carlsson's ability to provide strong leadership in favour of EU membership was weakened. In addition, the success of the anti-EU parties in the recent election also meant that the new Carlsson government was reliant upon their support in the *Riksdag*. The Social Democratic government therefore took a cautious line on the EU issue.

Public opinion polls also suggested that the electorate was evenly split on the membership issue and that the party campaigns would be instrumental in determining the referendum's outcome. Up until the last week of the referendum campaign, the 'No' side still maintained a slim lead. It was now that the 'Yes' campaign started to take the ascendancy and even then a series of negative opinion polls were still evident on 11 November.[43] It was so close that if the referendum had taken place ten days before, a 'No' vote would have been the probable outcome.

At the risk of seeming slow and indecisive, Carlsson adopted a low key approach. He allowed the Social Democratic party to fund and run two campaigns, one of which was led by the two anti-EU campaigners in his Cabinet. It was only in the last week, when the vote was looking too close to call that Carlsson became more assertive and galvanised the 'Yes' campaign. On the 8 November, he and his finance minister, Göran Persson, warned that a negative vote would damage the government's efforts to control the budget deficit and lead to a run on the Swedish currency.[44]

It was economic arguments, such as providing new sources of employment, injecting liberalisation into an overly regulated economy and consolidating governmental policies dealing with the budgetary deficit that were the main elements of the 'Yes' campaign. The pro-EU campaign linked together the EU as an international solution for Sweden's short-term domestic economic problems with the argument that Sweden must fully participate in EU decision-making if its long-term future was to be secured.

The 'No' campaign was mainly centred around the Greens, the Left Unity party and the anti-EU Social Democrats. The issues were more political and emotional. They ranged from the argument that EU membership would undermine Swedish democracy, that it would lead to a major reduction in Swedish social provisions and environmental standards, to being a direct attack on 'Swedishness', women's rights and the concept of Nordic cooperation. The 'No' campaign found that concerns over Sweden's open government and consensual democracy were especially influential with sceptical voters. However, to a large extent, the issue of Swedish security policy remained overshadowed by the economic priorities.[45] Sweden's non-alignment played only a relatively minor role in the debate, reflecting perhaps its declining importance on the Swedish political agenda. The severe recession between 1990-93 meant that, ultimately, the electorate placed economic recovery above all else.

The referendum campaign seemed to be perceived as a battle between the established government, parties and industrial lobbies and the more fringe elements of Swedish society. In the later stages of the campaign, Swedish industry mobilised itself and entered the debate on a large-scale. On 22 October, the four executives of Sweden's largest forestry firms, Stora,

SAC, Mood and Assidoman issued a joint statement calling for a 'Yes' vote in order to secure the prosperity of Swedish exports and business.[46] Indeed, the day before the vote Carlsson and Bildt joined forces in a rare show of unity and appealed for a positive outcome in a final television debate. They jointly argued that EU membership was now vital to the Swedish economy and hardly mentioned security issues at all.[47]

A brief survey of the referendum results

On the 13 November 1994, Sweden voted by 52.27 per cent against 46.83 per cent (with 0.9 per cent blank votes) in favour of joining the EU (see Table 5.1). Turnout averaged 83.32 per cent across 29 regional constituencies. Although the vote was positive, it was hardly an overwhelming endorsement of EU membership. 2.833 million people voted for EU membership (with 2.539 million voting against) out of a total voting population of 6.510 million people (see Table 5.2).

Table 5.1 Result of the 1994 Swedish referendum

Response	Percentage
No	46.83
Yes	52.27
Blank	0.90

Source: Swedish Embassy, London.

In reality though, the vote was carried on a regional constituency basis, with seventeen regional constituencies approving membership with twelve voting against (See Table 5.3). More importantly, the more populous, southern and urban regions, such as Stockholms Kommun (522,805 voters) and Stockholms Iän (694,000 voters) voted decisively in favour - by 61 per cent in both cases. These two constituencies alone accounted for 623,000 of the 2.8 million voters who approved of EU membership in the referendum. The three constituencies of Malmö representing another 310,000. In total, the seven combined constituencies of Stockholm, Malmö and Gothenburg accounted for 1.1 million of the 2.8 million 'Yes' votes (see Table 5.2).   Ultimately, the 'Yes' vote was carried by the southern, urban areas and in particular, the three main cities of Stockholm, Malmö and Gothenburg.

Table 5.2 Outcome of the 1994 Swedish referendum

Constituency	Yes	%	No	%	Blank	%	Void	Electorate	Turnout %
Stockholms kommun	263,836	61.5	161,198	37.6	3,968	0.9	250	522,805	82.11
Stockholms län	359,660	61.4	220,437	37.7	5,279	0.9	241	694,175	84.36
Uppsala län	92,167	53.4	78,636	45.6	1,852	1.1	92	205,736	83.97
Södermanlands län	86,083	53.8	72,430	45.3	1,533	2.0	95	191,199	83.76
Östergötlands län	139,697	53.9	116,689	45.0	2,791	1.0	135	309,509	83.78
Jönköpings län	95,009	48.5	99,451	50.7	1,644	0.8	100	230,987	84.94
Kronobergs län	58,015	51.4	53,824	47.6	1,141	1.0	39	134,559	83.99
Kalmar län	73,207	48.3	76,987	50.8	1,389	0.9	66	184,802	82.06
Gotlands län	17,996	50.9	17,017	48.1	364	1.0	22	43,878	80.68
Blekinge län	45,098	46.5	51,065	52.6	898	0.9	45	116,586	83.29
Kristianstads län	102,012	56.7	76,220	42.4	1,569	0.9	105	221,437	81.24
Malmö kommun	94,200	66.5	46,339	32.7	1,187	0.8	84	177,266	80.00
Malmöhus läns norra	94,921	61.3	58,724	37.9	1,246	0.8	99	190,087	81.54
Malmöhus läns södra	131,434	66.5	64,413	32.6	1,955	1.0	111	230,020	86.04
Hallands län	97,222	57.8	69,151	41.1	1,783	1.1	89	197,757	85.08
Göteborgs kommun	149,782	56.3	113,726	42.8	2,405	0.9	144	324,323	82.03
Bohuslän	101,999	51.1	95,979	48.1	1,723	0.9	121	233,940	85.42

Table 5.2 continued

Älvsbörgs län norra	75,611	46.5	85,643	52.6	1,479	0.9	64	193,716	84.04
Älvsbörgs län sodra	57,898	51.0	54,564	48.0	1,152	1.0	60	136,169	83.48
Skaraborgs län	86,364	49.5	86,177	49.4	1,876	1.1	82	208,908	83.53
Värmlands län	84,627	47.1	93,703	52.1	1,478	0.8	67	217,170	82.83
Örebro län	81,423	47.0	90,109	52.0	1,665	1.0	89	208,184	83.24
Vastmanlands län	87,058	54.3	71,778	44.8	1,448	0.9	76	193,184	83.03
Kopparbergs län	71,253	38.7	111,150	60.4	1,552	0.8	92	220,141	83.60
Gävleborgs län	74,767	41.3	104,583	57.8	1,542	0.9	88	222,780	81.24
Västernorrlands län	69,582	41.7	96,233	57.6	1,163	0.7	103	201,394	82.96
Jämtlands län	24,714	27.7	63,731	71.5	650	0.7	26	104,798	85.04
Västerbottens län	69,582	41.7	96,233	57.6	1,127	0.7	49	193,374	84.05
Norrbottens län	58,015	34.8	107,891	64.6	1,038	0.6	63	201,171	83.02
Total	**2,833,721**	**52.3**	**2,539,132**	**46.8**	**48,937**	**0.9**	**2697**	**6,510,055**	**83.32**

In contrast, northern Sweden voted overwhelmingly against EU membership.   Nine out of the ten, most northern provinces (from Norbotten in the far north down to Örebro) voted against and, in most cases, with large majorities, for example, Jämtlands voted with a huge majority of 71 per cent against membership (the largest majority either way in all of Sweden).   However, the main problem for the 'No' campaign was that the areas that voted against EU membership with sizeable majorities (six having anti-EU majorities of over 57 per cent), also tended to be those with low population density.

Table 5.3 Results of the 1994 Swedish referendum by constituency

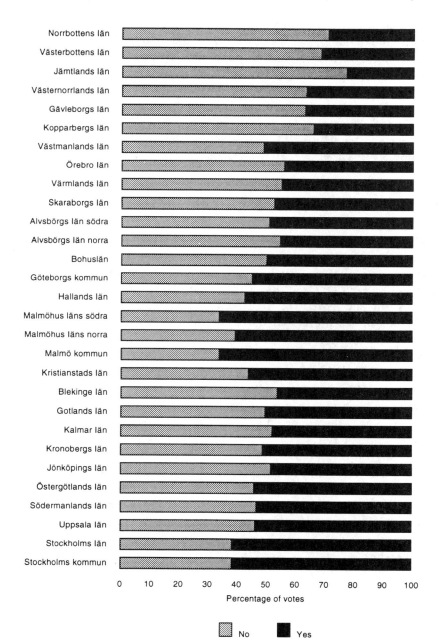

Their votes were easily offset by the more populous 'Yes'-voting constituencies of the South.   For example, the combined northern constituencies of Norbotten, Västerbotten, Jämtlands and Västernorrlands (which incidentally were those with the largest majorities against membership) were only equal in population size to one of the 'Yes' voting constituencies of Stockholm (Stockholms Kommun).   In terms of regional constituencies, the referendum was numerically won in the more marginal areas of Sweden's south east and south west.   For example, the regions of Kalmar (48.2 per cent-50.7 per cent against), Jönköping (48.5 per cent-50.7 per cent against), Alveborgs läns södra, (50.9 per cent-48 per cent for) and Skaraborgs län (49.5 per cent-49.4 per cent for).

The lessons of the Swedish EU membership referendum

There are several important lessons to be drawn from the referendum. Geography, class and political sympathies were deciding factors in how people voted.   Factors, such as sex, age and employment played less of a role.   In geographic terms, there were clear north-south, urban-rural divides on the Swedish EU membership issue.   The large anti-EU majorities in the north will mean that although the Carlsson government may have won the election, it will still be very sensitive to a large amount of vocal domestic opposition.

As a rule, the class vote seems to have been very strong.   In general, those in paid employment and students voted 'Yes' to the EU, whereas the unemployed and those working from home voted against in large numbers. In short, it was the educated and the better off who expected to gain from membership.   Civil servants and entrepreneurs proved to be two of the strongest groups in favour and voted in large numbers for membership (see Table 5.4).   Also and in complete contrast to their Finnish counterparts, there was a heavy preponderance of 'Yes' votes amongst Swedish farmers, especially in the south.   This suggests that the large geographical 'No' vote in the north was not entirely due to the area's reliance on farming, but indicates a wider rural and even provincial-based opposition to membership.

Table 5.4 Voting outcome of the 1994 Swedish referendum by class/professional group

Class/Professional Group	Yes	No	Blank
Paid employment	53	46	1
Unemployed	39	61	0
Early retirement	48	51	1
Working from home	39	61	0
Students	55	44	1

Source: Swedish Embassy, London.

In terms of political allegiance then, party members and sympathizers tended to follow party lines (see Table 5.5a and 5.5b). Those voters who sympathised with the parties on the Left, generally voted against membership, such as the Greens and Left Party members and voters. There was also a large majority of non-socialist party supporters who voted for membership, for example, some 86 per cent of Moderates voted in favour of membership (see Table 5.5a). Those who voted 'Yes' were mainly higher income supporters of the right-of-centre political parties.

The centre ground was far more splintered. About half of the Social Democratic supporters voted 'No' (49 per cent - see Table 5.5a), especially those in blue-collar work. Of the Centre's supporters, the majority voted against membership. The dividing line was presumably between the large farmers in the south (who voted 'Yes') and the small farmers in the north, who voted against membership.

Table 5.5a Voting outcome of the 1994 Swedish referendum by political bias

Political bias	Yes	No	Blank
Moderate Party	86	13	1
Liberal Party	81	18	1
Social Democrats	50	49	1
Centre Party	45	54	1
Christian Democrats	41	59	0
New Democracy	34	62	4
Green Party	15	84	1
Left Party	10	90	0

Source: Swedish Embassy, London.

Table 5.5b Voting outcome of the 1994 Swedish referendum by political stance

Left/Right	Yes	No	Blank
Far Right	31	69	0
Moderate Right	40	59	1
Centre	46	53	1
Moderate Left	75	24	1
Far Left	86	13	1

Source: Swedish Embassy, London.

In terms of age, opposition among first time voters (18-21 age group) was higher than expected. This may have reflected their general insecurity about Sweden's future, given its recent economic troubles. However, all the age groups over the age of 21 voted in favour (see Table 5.6). Most women however, voted against (by 52 per cent - see Table 5.7). This can be at least partially attributed to their heavy reliance on the Swedish public sector for employment and services and reflected their concerns that EU membership would undermine their social rights. In particular, women between 22 and 64 voted against and this was reversed in the same groups for Swedish men (see Table 5.8). Despite the government's arguments about reforming the system through EU membership, many women feared that the Swedish welfare system would be under threat from EU membership.

Table 5.6 Voting outcome of the 1994 Swedish referendum by age

Age	Yes	No	Blank
18 - 21	40	59	1
22 - 30	52	47	1
31 - 64	53	46	1
64 -	58	41	1

Source: Swedish Embassy, London.

Table 5.7 Voting outcome of the 1994 Swedish referendum by gender

Gender	Yes	No	Blank
Female	47	52	1
Male	57	42	1

Source: Swedish Embassy, London.

Table 5.8 Voting outcome of the 1994 Swedish referendum by age and gender

Age group	Females - Yes	Males - Yes
18 - 21	34	46
22 - 30	47	57
31 - 64	49	58
64 -	54	64

Source: Swedish Embassy, London.

Those elements that might be described as the most characteristically 'Nordic' part of the electorate, such as those dependent on the welfare system and those outside the large cities, rejected membership. Thus, the Carlsson government's problems with maintaining public support for EU membership look far from over. It will take a considerable time to alter domestic political attitudes and this problem still inhibits the freedom of manoeuvre of Swedish governments even after the country has become a full EU member.[48] It may also affect the ability of the government to completely drop its non-aligned stance regarding Swedish security policy in the future. It is to this dilemma and the nature of Sweden's role in the CFSP, that this chapter will now turn.

Sweden, Austria, Finland and the CFSP

The security policies of all three new EU members are, at this time, in a transitional period. Swedish security policy has, for example, undergone fundamental changes since 1989 and has been reduced to simply 'non-participation in military alliances'. It now reflects little of the previous pre-1989 doctrine of neutrality.[49]

In a similar vein, although Austria is still bound by its 1955 Federal Constitutional Act (which ensures her permanent neutrality), she has moved a long way from her pre-1989 position. Austrian policy is now 'active' and seeks the establishment of more stable security mechanisms for Europe. Indeed, Austria may even soon be at the point of ditching neutrality if its government can gain sufficient parliamentary and public support for a revision of the 1955 Act.[50] Without doubt, Austria clearly sees the EU as providing the most credible security option for Europe in the future.[51]

This view is also shared by Finland, who perhaps most of all, perceives her security interests as being linked to the future development of the CFSP, especially given her proximity to a rather unstable post-communist Russia. Arter, for example, has recently argued that Finland's approval of membership in her 1994 referendum was, in part, a vote for the West and a future CFSP, rather than as a specific 'yes' to the economic aspects of the Maastricht Treaty, such as EMU.[52] Indeed, Finnish neutrality has radically changed. Not only did it move from 'semi-mandatory' to voluntary status with the replacement of the 1948 Treaty, but it has, as in the Swedish case, been fundamentally reduced to just military non-alliance. Finnish policy is no longer 'passive' and Finland, perhaps the most of all three new EU members, has moved to actively promoting deeper political and security cooperation because of her fear of future instability in Russia.[53]

At face value, the movement of Austria and Finland away from traditional neutral stances seems to be more radical than in the Swedish case, as their neutrality carried with it international legal recognition. None the less, once the exogenous pressures of a Cold War Europe declined, the legal status of their neutrality became less appropriate or relevant and much easier to revise without provoking international controversy or intervention. It also reflects the fact that both Austria and Finland are geographically closer to, and in many cases actually border, those areas most affected by the post-1989 changes. They are, therefore, most keen to see a more stable security framework develop in order to fill the political vacuum left around their borders by the break-up of the bloc division of Europe.

Yet, Sweden, Austria and Finland now face a common challenge. They have to recognise that the European security agenda is no longer being prioritised by the 'exogenous' forces of a bloc-division of Europe or the common threat of communist Soviet Union challenging western Europe, but rather by 'endogenous forces' inside western Europe. More specifically, the new challenge confronting the European neutrals arises from deeper European integration pushing forward cooperation in foreign and defence matters.

Indeed, there are striking similarities in the three countries' approaches to the CFSP. All three have accepted on the one hand, the principles, content and future development of the CFSP and have even consented to participating in NATO's 'Partnership for Peace' initiative and on the other, all three have chosen to be only observers within the Western European

Union (WEU). The basic dilemma here is that the Union's CFSP still remains embryonic and simultaneously accompanies the transitional phases within the three neutral countries' respective security policies. In reality, it is not difficult for the three countries to agree to becoming full and active members of the CFSP as it remains, at this point, mostly undeveloped.

Article J.1 is careful to refer to 'the Union and its member states' in defining and implementing a CFSP, signalling its intergovernmental nature. The general commitments outlined in Article J.1, such as, to safeguard common values and fundamental interests and preserving peace and international security in accordance with the UN, are already practised by the three new EU members. In 1994, for instance, Sweden committed a stand-by brigade to the UN's peacekeeping forces. In June 1995, Carl Bildt was appointed as the EU's chief mediator for the former Yugoslavia.

Nor is the concept of systematic cooperation objectionable to the three neutrals, as long as the Council remains the body responsible for deciding 'joint actions' and will continue to do so by unanimity. It is only on procedural questions and in the process of developing and adopting joint actions that qualified majority voting can then be used. Their national security interests can be protected, especially as the CFSP now includes four member states committed to a policy of military non-alliance.[54] In practice, the CFSP is not a military alliance as it stands and will be an incremental process. The 1996 IGC will primarily deal with improving the CFSP's ability to deal with short-term crisis management, which all three new members perceive as beneficial. However, the three neutral countries broadly share common objections to the CFSP and therefore, it is most useful to examine Sweden's position, which in comparative terms, seems the least likely to drop its stance of military non-alliance at the moment.

Areas of Swedish concern

The first area of Swedish concern revolves around the CFSP's institutional arrangements. Under Article J.4.4 of the TEU, the EU has virtually subcontracted 'decisions and actions of the Union which have defence implications'.[55] Consequently, the Swedish government has argued that any defence arrangements will be developed through the WEU and it is WEU membership, and not CFSP participation, that is problematical for her security policy. Sweden (along with Austria and Finland) only took up observer status of the WEU in January 1995 as this allowed her to participate in discussions on peace-keeping, but did not involve any military obligations.

In practice, the problem for the Swedish (but also Austrian and Finnish) governments lies in the fact that the WEU fulfils three roles. First, it is an existing west European security arrangement. Although the WEU may not be a full-scale military alliance, as in the case of NATO, it does include collective security guarantees (Article V) in its 1948 Treaty. This, of course, should contravene Sweden's position on military non-alliance. Secondly, it represents the CFSP's embryonic defence organ and formally links the EU and WEU memberships in defence cooperation. Thirdly, it acts as the *de facto* 'European pillar' of NATO and thus, for the Swedes, implies that full WEU membership also includes the acceptance of an associated role within NATO; again contravening Sweden's 'non-participation in military alliances'. Consequently, in April 1995, the Swedish government reaffirmed that it had no plans to become a full WEU or NATO member for the foreseeable future.

This, of course, may prove to be a short-term problem for the three new EU members. Both the WEU and NATO are also experiencing a period of transition and may be expanded to include members from central and eastern Europe. In addition, the WEU's 1948 Treaty is due to expire in 1998 and this could provide an opportunity for removing the WEU's collective defence guarantees; thereby reducing the costs associated with joining. Moreover, as the CFSP, WEU and NATO will mostly be dealing with crisis management issues during the 1990s, this provides new opportunities for cooperation between the three new EU members, the WEU and NATO. Certainly, Sweden is now more inclined to work in WEU and NATO-led projects. For example, from May 1995, Sweden participated in the WEU police force in Mostar and in late 1995, Swedish troops were included within NATO's peace implementation force (I-FOR) in Bosnia.

However, although Sweden has recently tended to follow the EU lead in security matters - for instance, in the process of recognising new European states, such as Macedonia[56] - the Swedes are generally cautious regarding the medium-term development of the CFSP. In particular, the Swedish government is concerned about two potential areas of development provided for under Article J.4 of the TEU, which stipulates that the CFSP will include 'all questions related to the security of the Union, including the eventual framing of a common defence policy, which might in time lead to a common defence'.

According to Carlsson, an EU common defence policy could be problematic as 'Sweden's non-participation in military alliances, with the aim of making it possible to be neutral in the event of war....remains unchanged'.[57]   However, Sweden's security policy has already been treated flexibly in the recent past.   For example, Sweden has, since September 1994, agreed to participate in NATO's 'Partnership For Peace' initiative, on the grounds that it was a confidence building measure and included the central and eastern European states.

However, it is generally perceived that an EU common defence policy is the first step towards creating an eventual common defence and thus, Sweden's participation will depend on its form and in particular, whether it will require collective security guarantees (especially from the outset). These would be difficult for Sweden to adhere to given the problems that her government faces in maintaining domestic support.   Consequently, in May 1995, the Swedish government rejected the possibility that the CFSP should include a 'Mutual Assistance' clause.

Furthermore, the longer-term prospect of creating 'an eventual common defence' is treated sceptically by the Swedes.   The concept is, of course, open to many interpretations, from limited collective security guarantees to fully fledged, integrated European defence forces.   However, for the most part, any integrated EU common defence is still too ambitious for the incremental nature of Swedish security policy.   According to Swedish Foreign Minister Lena Hjelm-Wallen in January 1995, the Social Democratic government's security policy has three elements.   Firstly, that her government believes that decisive steps towards a common defence would not be taken at the 1996 IGC.   Secondly, if these steps were taken then Sweden would not participate in binding defence cooperation.   Thirdly, that Sweden would not obstruct other EU members from seeking common defence.[58]   Implicit within Swedish governmental thinking, is the assumption that a multi-tier development of the CFSP is likely and acceptable.

There are numerous problems with the Swedish position and there is still a high level of ambiguity regarding Swedish policy towards the emerging CFSP.   This partly reflects the declining domestic consensus between the main political parties on the future of Sweden's security policy.   If a multi-party consensus is still required on security policy, then the cautious attitude of the Centre Party towards the notion of abandoning non-alignment remains a barrier and will need to be accommodated.   The Social Democratic government, on 22 February 1995, again outlined its reluctance to be part of a permanent European defence force and formally stated that

Sweden 'must not lead other states to expect Swedish military involvement in the event of an armed conflict. Sweden neither needs nor wishes to impose restrictions on itself'.[59]

However, since May 1995, the government has again seemed to soften its position regarding the CFSP and looks as if it could make some minor concessions at the forthcoming 1996 IGC. In May, Lena Hjelm-Wallen suggested that the CFSP should be strengthened at the 1996 IGC and that there was a need to 'take a long, hard look at the consensus requirement' for CFSP action.[60] Otherwise, further enlargement would undermine the capacity of the EU to deal with external problems. The Swedish government did, however, declare that there was no question of Sweden supporting the abolition of the right of veto where vital national security interests were at stake, but would consider modifications to the CFSP (such as qualified majority voting) for minor security issues.[61] The real problem for the EU and Sweden is determining who decides whether the issues are of vital or only of minor national interest. Clearly, Sweden, Austria and Finland would prefer the CFSP to remain primarily intergovernmental.

Yet, if the ambiguities in the Swedish position are to be removed, then the EU must also take action. It must further define its security responsibilities and needs to clarify the relationship between the 'Atlanticist' defence of NATO and the CFSP's future common defence. Thus, the Swedish position, despite being somewhat ambiguous, will remain until the relationship between the EU, CFSP, WEU and NATO is more clearly defined. Officially, Sweden will continue to remain for the most part, an aloof observer, while at the practical level it will cooperate as part of the CFSP on a selective basis. In reality, it is more likely that Finland and Austria will become full CFSP members before Sweden.

Conclusion

Overall, Waite's arguments that Swedish EU policy included separate economic and political considerations appear to be no longer relevant. By the late 1980s, these considerations could no longer be separated in practical terms. Since the strategic changes in Europe, Swedish security policy has been more flexibly defined as having a European identity and as being restricted to non-participation in alliances.

The recent EU referendum also illustrates that perceptions of Swedish non-alignment and neutrality are changing. The traditional domestic consensus on security policy amongst the main political parties has disappeared, with the Social Democrats preferring to maintain non-alignment and the Moderates wishing to abandon it. The role of the Centre Party is also of relevance here. At this moment, it favours the maintenance of a nominal non-aligned position for Sweden and this will make comprehensive party consensus more difficult. This in itself creates domestic friction over and within Swedish security policy. However, the EU referendum also illustrates that the domestic importance of Swedish security policy has declined. Differences in policy are now possible between the parties as the issue is no longer the main priority. Economic issues were more dominant than security aspects during the referendum campaigns. None the less, the challenge of Sweden's future role in the emerging CFSP will ensure that security issues will remain problematic for the Swedish government in the short-term and will not be completely removed from her political agenda.

Notes

1.   For the purposes of this chapter, the author has decided to ignore Norway for two reasons. First, Norway is not a neutral country and consequently, does not share many of the security dilemmas that confront Austria, Finland and Sweden as neutrals. Secondly, although Norway did negotiate an accession deal, the country rejected EU membership in its 1994 referendum and therefore, does not participate in the CFSP.

2.   The term, 'EFTA neutral' applies to Austria, Finland and Sweden in this context as Switzerland (the other EFTA neutral) did not participate in the 1993-95 EU accession round.

3.   See Nelsen, B. (ed.), Norway and the European Community, Westview, Boulder, 1993.

4.   Jessop, P.C. and Deàk, F., *The Origins of Neutrality: Its History, Economics and Law,* New York, 1976.

5.   Hakovirta, H., *East-West Conflict and European Neutrality,* Clarendon Press, Oxford, 1988, p. 8.

6.   Frei, D., *Dimensionen neutraler Politik: Ein Beitrag zur Theorie der internationalen Beziehungen* (Geneva), 1969, pp. 103-47.

7.   Op cit, Hakovirta (1988), p. 5.

8.   Ibid, pp. 28-29.

9.   Sundelius, B. (ed), *The Committed Neutral,* Westview Press, Boulder, p. 1.

10. Goldmann, K., 'The Swedish Model of Security Policy' in *Understanding the Swedish Model,* edited by J-E Lane, Frank Cass, London, 1991, p. 124.

11. Miljan, T., *The Reluctant Europeans,* Hurst & Co, London, 1977.

12. Strom, K., 'Norway, Sweden and the New Europe', *Scandinavian Political Studies,* Fall 1992, vol. 64, no. 4, p. 506.

13. Kruzel, J., 'Sweden's Security Dilemma: Balancing Domestic Realities with the Obligations of Neutrality' in B. Sundelius (ed), *The Committed Neutral,* Westview Press, Boulder, 1989, pp. 67-93.

14. Op cit, Goldmann (1991), p. 129.

15. Archer, C., 'Conflict Prevention in Europe: The Case of the Nordic States and Macedonia' *Cooperation and Conflict,* vol. 29, no. 4, 1995, pp. 367-86.

16. *Debate of Foreign Affairs,* Ministry of Foreign Affairs, Stockholm, 22 February 1995, p. 6.

17. Jankowitsch, P. and Hannes, P., 'The Process of European Integration and Neutral Austria' in S. Harden (ed), *Neutral States and the European Community,* Brassey's, London, 1994, p. 45.

18. Zamanek, K., 'Austria's Policy of Neutrality: Constants and Variables' in H. Neuhold and H. Thalberg (eds), *The European Neutrals in International Affairs,* Westview Press, Boulder, 1984, pp. 18-19.

19. Waite, J., 'The Swedish Paradox: EEC and Neutrality' *Journal of Common Market Studies,* no. 12, 1973, pp. 319-36.

20. See Arter, D., *The Politics of European Integration in the Twentieth Century,* Aldershot, Dartmouth, 1993, p. 222.

21. Ministry of Foreign Affairs, *On Sweden and the European Economic Community,* 18 March 1971, UD, Stockholm, p. 4.

22. Op cit, Arter, D. (1993), p. 223.

23. Commission of the ECs, *Europe Information - External Relations* 48/81 Commission of the ECs, Brussels, 1981.

24. Hamilton, C., *The Nordic EFTA Countries' Options: Seeking Community Membership or a Permanent EEA Accord,* Discussion Paper 524, CEPR, London, 1991, p. 1.

25. For a more detailed explanation see Kruzel, J. (1989) op cit, pp. 74-9.

122 *The 1995 enlargement of the European Union*

26. Dörfer, I., 'Swedish Security Policy Facing the Future', *Tio debattinlägg om svensk säkerhetspolitik,* Folk & Försvar, Kalmar, 1985.

27. Miles, L., 'Enlargement of the European Union and the Nordic Model', *Journal of European Integration,* vol. XIX, no. 1, March 1996, pp. 245-59.

28. Ministry of Foreign Affairs, *Sweden, the EC and Security Policy Developments in Europe,* 2, UD, Stockholm, 1991, p. 14.

29. Huldt, B., 'Sweden and European-Community Building 1945-92' in S. Harden (ed), *Neutral States and the European Community,* Brassey's, London, 1994, pp. 120-1.

30. Commission of the ECs, *Sweden's Application For Membership: Opinion of the EC,* SEC (92) 1528 FINAL, 7 August 1992, Commission of the ECs, Brussels, p. 25.

31. Svensson, S., 'Social Democrats Return To Power', *Current Sweden,* 404, Swedish Institute, Stockholm, 1994, p. 5.

32. Karvonen, L. and Sundelius, B., 'The Nordic Neutrals: Facing the European Union' in Miles, L. (ed), *The European Union and the Nordic Countries,* Routledge, London, 1996, pp. 245-59.

33. Ministry of Foreign Affairs, *Statement by Mr Ulf Dinkelspiel, Minister For European Affairs and Foreign Trade at the Opening of Sweden's Accession Negotiations,* 1 February 1993, UD, Stockholm, p. 5.

34. Miles, L., The 1993-1994 Enlargement Negotiations, *European Access,* 3 June 1994, Commission of the ECs, Cardiff, pp. 8-11.

35. Op cit, Dinkelspiel, U. (1993), p. 5.

36. Miles, L., *The 1993-1994 Enlargement Negotiations - A Critical Appraisal,* Discussion Paper 1/94, CEUS, Hull, p. 12.

37. Ministry of Foreign Affairs, *The Swedish Contribution To The Community Budget,* Position Paper, Chapter 27, UD, Stockholm, 1993, p. 1.

38. Milner, H., *Sweden - Social Democracy in Practice,* OUP, Oxford, 1989.

39. Op cit, Dinkelspiel, U. (1993), p. 4.

40. Miles, L., 'The European Union and the Nordic Countries: Impacts on the Integration Process' in C. Rhodes and S. Mazey (eds), *The State of the European Community, Volume III: Building a European Polity?* Longman/Lynne Reiner, London, 1995, pp. 317-34.

41. Op cit, Svensson, S. (1994), p. 5.

42.   Carlsson, I., *Statement of Government Policy by the Prime Minister to the Swedish Parliament,* 7 October 1994, Stockholm, p. 3.

43.   *The Financial Times,* 'Swedes Reminded That Quisling was pro-Europe', 11 November 1994, p. 3.

44.   *The Financial Times,* 'Swedish Leaders Plead EU Cause', 8 November 1994, p. 2.

45.   See Kokko, A., 'Sweden: Effects of EU Membership' *The World Economy,* vol. 17, no. 5, September 1994, pp. 667-77.

46.   *The Financial Times,* 'Swedish Forestry Companies Join Forces to Urge EU Membership', 22 October 1994, p. 2.

47.   *The Financial Times,* 'Swedish Political Rivals Unite To Call For Yes Vote on EU', 12 November 1994, p. 1.

48.   Swedish opinion polls in 1995 consistently showed that public opinion had turned against EU membership. In July 1995, opinion polls indicated that 61 per cent of Swedes were now against EU membership. In general, the pro-EU parties also did badly in the September 1995 European parliamentary election - Miles, L. and Kintis, A., 'The New Member States: Sweden, Austria and Finland' in J. Lodge (ed), *The 1994 Elections To The European Parliament,* Pinter, London 1995, pp. 227-36.

49.   See Sundelius, B., 'Changing Course: When Neutral Sweden Chose To Join the European Community' in Carlsnaes, W. and Smith, S. (eds), *European Foreign Policy: The EC and Changing Perspectives in Europe,* SAGE, London, 1994, pp. 177-201.

50.   Phinnemore, D., 'Austria in the European Union - Saying Farewell To Neutrality?' in J. Lovenduski and J. Stanyer (ed), *Contemporary Political Studies, Volume One,* PSA/ Short-Run Press, Belfast, 1995, pp. 363-70.

51.   Koch, K., 'Austria: The Economic Logic of Accession' in J. Redmond (ed), *Prospective Europeans,* Harvester-Wheatsheaf, London, 1994, pp. 45-6.

52.   Arter, D., 'The EU Referendum in Finland on 16 October 1994: A Vote for the West, not for Maastricht' *Journal of Common Market Studies,* vol. 33, no. 3, 1995, pp. 361-88.

53.   Ministry of Foreign Affairs, *Security in a Changing World,* UM, Helsinki.

54.   These are, of course, Austria, Finland, Ireland and Sweden.

55.   Salmon, T., *The Common Foreign and Security Policy and Defence,* Discussion Paper of the Jean Monnet Group of Experts, CEUS, Hull, 1995.

56. Mouritzen, H., 'The Two Musterknaben and the Naughty Boy: Sweden, Finland and Denmark in the Process of European Integration' *Cooperation and Conflict,* vol. 28, no. 4, 1993, pp. 373-402.

57. Ministry of Foreign Affairs, *Statement of Government Policy Presented by the Prime Minister to the Swedish Parliament,* 7 October 1994, UD, Stockholm, p. 13.

58. Ministry of Foreign Affairs, *Address by the Minister For Foreign Affairs at the National Conference of the People and Defence Federation,* 31 January 1995, UD, Stockholm, p. 2.

59. Ministry of Foreign Affairs, *Statement of Government Policy Presented at the Parliamentary Debate on Foreign Affairs,* 22 February 1995, UD, Stockholm, p. 3.

60. Ministry of Foreign Affairs, *Towards a New European Security Order - A Swedish View,* 30 May 1995, UD, Stockholm, p. 10.

61. Ministry of Foreign Affairs, *The EU Intergovernmental Conference 1996 - Government Report to the Riksdag,* UD, Stockholm, 30, p. 56.

6 Finland and Agriculture

DAVID ARTER

Shortly after the Soviet Union was formally pronounced dead on 25 December 1991 - or perhaps more correctly stated 'brain-dead', since many of the old Soviet organs continued to function[1] - the 1948 Friendship, Cooperation and Mutual Assistance (FCMA) Treaty with the USSR, which had been the cornerstone of Finland's post-war foreign policy, was allowed to lapse and on 18 March 1992 Finland applied for membership of the European Union (EU). So long as the USSR remained in existence, neutrality, which in essence denoted no military cooperation with the Soviet Union, represented the main component in Finland's security policy and maintaining amicable relations with the Kremlin was of paramount importance. Precisely as in Sweden, neutrality had been viewed as the manifest constraint on full membership of an EU which has as its long-term goal the ever closer union of its peoples, viz political union. However, the more Finno-Soviet trade crumbled, the higher the economic costs of neutrality became and the greater the importance of securing freer access to west European markets. Viewed in this light, the final collapse of the old Cold War security system provided rationalisation, rather than a fundamental rationale for an EU application.

The road to Brussels

The events moulding the New Europe of post-1989 undermined Finland's stable position between western Europe and the Soviet Union and challenged her to demonstrate a capacity for adaptation. In particular, with her Ostpolitik, both its security and mercantile components overtaken by events, Finland was effectively obliged to define and pursue a new Westpolitik - that is, to reconsider her position in relation to a range of Western institutions inter alia the European Free Trade Association (EFTA), the proposed European Economic Area (EEA), the EU and even the North Atlantic Treaty Organisation (NATO).

The disintegration of the Communist empire in eastern Europe, following the autumn revolutions of 1989, and the subsequent collapse of the Soviet Union itself, fundamentally altered Finland's geopolitical position. Finland ceased to be a frontier state in the ideological-military sense of being an outpost of Western pluralist democracy bordering the Communist superpower. Rather, the security architecture of the Baltic took on an aspect reminiscent of the inter-war years. Finland was flanked to the east by the Russian Federation which, whilst still a military force (if not an actual threat to the West), was a state whose destiny appeared uncertain. To the south, the Baltic successor states re-emerged as sovereign entities, although Russian army and naval troops remained stationed on their territory. To the west, the so-called 'Nordic balance' was disturbed: Sweden remained armed and neutral, but Danish and Norwegian membership of NATO became strategically less significant in the post-Cold War climate and as NATO evolved and assumed new forms such as the consultative North Atlantic Cooperation Council (NACC).

The central pillar of Finnish post-war foreign and security policy was the 1948 FCMA which specified that 'in the event of Finland, or the Soviet Union through Finland, becoming the object of an armed attack by Germany, or any other state allied with the latter, Finland will...fight to repel the attack'. Two crises in post-war Finno-Soviet relations, particularly the 'Note Crisis' of 1961, suggested that Finland never fully grasped the Kremlin's almost obsessional concern about a possible resurgence of German militarism.[2] Although falling clearly within the Soviet sphere of influence, Finland gradually sought strategic autonomy by proclaiming its independence as a neutral state - a neutrality which could trace its origins to the pre-war era. It was a neutrality which did not rest on legal specification - the preamble to the FCMA treaty alluded only generally to 'Finland's desire to remain outside the conflicting interests of the great powers' - but simply on a unilateral statement of intent by the Finns backed by skilful diplomacy. For the Finns, neutrality became very much the art of the possible, the credibility of the policy resting in large part on the extent of its recognition by the Kremlin.

In fact, Moscow was generally reluctant to recognize Finnish neutrality, at least until the late 1960s. It was 1957 before the term was first officially used in a joint communiqué on a Soviet visit to Finland, although on the twelfth anniversary of the FCMA in 1960 Pravda described the treaty as 'an international juridical document which confirms Finnish neutrality'.[3] The period of détente between the Superpowers in the late 1960s, however, heralded a more amenable Soviet attitude towards Finnish neutrality, conditioned in no small measure by the Kremlin's perception of the service Finland could perform as an envoy in furthering her goals. Finland, in short, was encouraged to canvass international support for an agenda which had been mutually agreed and vetted in Moscow. It was no coincidence that Helsinki staged the initial round of Strategic Arms Limitations (SALT) Talks in 1970 and the Conference on Security and Cooperation in Europe (CSCE) five years later. In turn, Finland achieved global recognition for what President Urho Kekkonen (1956-81) described as a policy of active neutrality.

When, however, in a speech in Finlandia House, in Helsinki, during the 'revolutionary autumn' of 1989, Gorbachev declared that 'Finland is a neutral Nordic country' - the first Soviet leader publicly to recognise the fact - there was already a sense in which it appeared he was seeking to discourage Finland from embarking on a policy of overt Western alignment which by then the Kremlin was largely helpless to prevent. Gorbachev in sum seemed to be appealing to Finland to maintain the 'old order' viz her neutrality and special relationship with the Kremlin at the very time the disintegration of the Soviet empire in eastern Europe heralded the start of a new epoch on the continent.

In geo-economic rather than geopolitical terms, in contrast, Finland's position in the nascent New Europe remained basically unchanged. As a prosperous market economy (albeit one by 1992 experiencing severe recession), it stood at the economic frontier between the western Europe of the rich and the eastern Europe of the poor. The re-emergent Baltic states, to be sure, offered fresh trading possibilities and the prospect of a cheap, but relatively skilled labour force. However, the demise of the Soviet Union and attendant collapse of Finno-Soviet trade dictated the need for Finland, as an exporting nation, to find compensatory trade outlets - and that meant in practice looking for wider markets in western Europe.

In many ways, Finland's post-war economic development was unique: she made rapid progress as a Western manufacturing economy on the back of a close barter-trading relationship with her superpower neighbour. Ironically, the need to repay a war indemnity to Communist Russia, mainly in terms of heavy goods and machinery transformed an essentially agrarian economy and propelled Finland down the road of Western-style capitalism. A succession of five-year Finno-Soviet commercial agreements, moreover, which involved importing raw materials (mainly gas and oil) in return for the export of Western consumer durables, had an important counter-cyclical effect, buoying Finland against the worst effects of recession in the West.

By the late 1980s, Finland was a highly prosperous country, ranking higher in the OECD league of states by per capita income than Sweden, and with talk of the 'Japanisation' of its economy reflecting the extent of the 'economic miracle'. If 'overheating', in the form of an import-intensive consumer boom, led to a growing balance of payments deficit and if it was foreign borrowing which sustained investment in a modernised transport and communications infrastructure, unemployment remained low. One cloud only served as a precursor of the recessionary storm to come: the fall in oil prices in 1986 hit Finno-Soviet trade, and in reducing the volume of Finland's exports to Russia led many small and medium-sized textile firms into bankruptcy. Furthermore, Gorbachev's economic re-structuring or perestroika, which instituted the principle (though hardly the practice) of company-to-company dealing, further complicated trade with the Soviet Union.

Indeed, if perestroika was certainly no panacea for the Soviet economy, it proved, ironically, to be a real problem for the neighbouring Finnish one. This was because the concern of the Soviet reformists to attract foreign currency reserves on the back of more diversified oil exports to the West led to a substantial decline in Finno-Soviet trade. The less oil was piped to Finland, the lower the value of Finnish export goods to the Soviet Union. From a figure of 20 per cent in the early 1980s (it had touched 25 per cent in the 1970s), Finland's exports to the Soviet Union plummeted to under 5 per cent of her overall trade in 1990 - the year Moscow unilaterally announced a shift from barter arrangements to hard currency transactions. This took effect from 1 January 1991, and hence although the collapse of the USSR plainly complicated matters for Finland, it did not cause them. The pressure to 'westernise' her trade mounted throughout Gorbachev's fruitless pursuit of perestroika.

The first big Westward step was Finland's application to join the European Economic Space, subsequently the EEA, in 1990. The EEA represented a classic marriage of convenience: to accommodate the 'EFTA-neutrals, the EEA did not include agriculture, defence and certain elements of regional policy; so as not to retard the President of the European Commission Jacques Delors' concern for 'deepening' the integration within the Community it did not entail full membership status. A year before an EEA agreement was reached in November 1991, however, Sweden suddenly broke ranks and her Social Democratic Prime Minister, Ingvar Carlsson, blaming the protracted nature of the negotiations - but in reality to calm the turbulent financial markets - announced his country's intention of seeking full EU membership. In March 1992, with the Soviet Union dead and buried, the Finnish bourgeois majority government under Esko Aho followed suit. During a speech at the College of Europe in Bruges, moreover, President Mauno Koivisto went much further than Sweden (which presented a shopping list of conditions) by indicating Finland's readiness to accept the Maastricht Treaty on European Union in total.

Summing up, Finland's 'European policy' until the collapse of the Soviet Union was based on a search for an accommodation between the economic imperative of access, along with Norway and Sweden, to crucial Western export markets and the political imperative of preserving the credibility of her 'neutrality' and special relationship with the Kremlin. During the Cold War, the political imperative - and security policy considerations - necessarily took first priority and operated at the expense of economic dictates.[4] The EEA notion thus had the merit for Finland of facilitating her further economic integration into western Europe, whilst avoiding full membership of a 'Twelve' committed to political union. Such membership was ruled out by her policy of neutrality. Moscow's unilateral shift in 1990 to hard currency transactions, and the subsequent collapse of the Soviet Union (anticipated for about fifteen years in Finland), combined to strengthen the economic imperative of extending further into Western markets. Only three months after the demise of the USSR, Finland abandoned neutrality and applied for EU membership. Two months earlier, on 9 January, in a communication to parliament, the Finnish government stated its commitment to what was called the 'core of neutrality'; namely, military nonalignment and a credible national defence. This appeared largely for domestic consumption. Indeed, the 'core of neutrality' rhetoric was exposed as a sham when, in December 1993, Finland agreed to the Common Foreign and Security Policy (CFSP) commitment and actively endorsed the 'defence dimension' in the Maastricht Treaty.

The EU referendum

Following a clear 'yes' at the referendum on 16 October, Finland on 1 January 1995 became the first successor state of the inter-war period to become a full member of the EU. 57 per cent had voted in favour and 43 per cent against joining. For many voters the 'membership dividend' was perceived in expressive as much as incremental terms. In other words, membership would serve to anchor Finland to the west European mainstream and institutionalise her position as a member of a bloc of west European states to which she had belonged by dint of her politico-economic system, if not geography, from the earliest years of independence. It was a question of identity - Finland's identity in the New Europe.[5]

The EU debate in Finland was generally low-key. In the vanguard of the pro-membership lobby was big business which contended that economic necessity was the mother of accession. The forest industry, 80 per cent of whose exports went to the EU, well illustrates the point. As an EEA member it had been the victim of French protectionism and an orchestrated campaign against the import of cheaper and superior quality Finnish paper products. Consequently, it sought, via full membership, to participate in the formulation of an EU forestry policy (with regard to such key issues as clear-cutting, eco-labelling, regulations on growing forest and the controversy about the rightful balance between primary fibre and recycled input) and to avail itself of any research and development monies available. But the forest industry deployed two arguments extensively used by big business advocates of membership. First, although no industry in Finland would derive greater benefit from full membership - with Finland and Sweden in, the EU's forest resources would almost double - the damage of exclusion would be to the whole economy and the welfare structures that depend on its wealth generation. Second, EU membership would mean the final abolition of the 'Finland-added tax', so to speak, in that it would reduce the perceived politico-economic risk for outside investors. Membership, in short, would create conditions of trust and economic security and provide insurance against interference from Russia. It would give Finland a new reference point. The alternative scenario, it was intimated, was isolation, discrimination and loss of investment. In general, at a time of deep recession - 18.5 per cent unemployment and a massive state debt - the business lobby presented EU membership as a window of opportunity, if not exactly a panacea for Finland's economic maladies.

When confronted with opposition from the agricultural producers' organisation MTK and the farmers (discussed later), the EU proponents adopted an understanding but ultimately 'cruel to be kind' approach. Membership would contribute to promoting and expediting the structural changes in Finnish agriculture necessary for its long-term survival and in particular to ensuring a shift away from the present concentration on crop cultivation. In their defence, they could draw on the views of experts who were of the opinion that Finland's best prospects lay in the fields of beef and dairy farming - where the price differentials with the EU were smallest - along with a general diversification of production.

The political case for accession was two-pronged. First, membership would give Finland influence in the gestation and formulation of EU policy. It would be represented in the key decisional arenas - the Commission, Council of Ministers and European Council - in a way it would not as an EEA member. There was, it was pointed out, a tacit acceptance in west European capitals that each applicant state had its own national interests which it would continue to pursue and the challenge, therefore, would be to acquire the 'Euro-craft' (negotiating and alliance-building skills) with which to get the best deal for Finland.

The second political line, a crucial but essentially non-incremental one, held that the principal gain from EU membership lay in the way it would identify Finland once and for all as a mainstream west European state. Whilst this had a strong prima facie attraction for the younger generation, it was less certain to appeal to a middle-aged cohort which had tended to see Finland as a centre of Europe, especially as Helsinki had staged the inaugural CSCE in 1975.

There were those in the 'yes' camp who, whilst attracted by the prospect of a clear Western identity, did not share the unequivocal enthusiasm of the big business lobby and its 'wider markets, increased investment, economies of scale' vindication. Theirs was a critical acceptance of the case for accession which, crudely stated, wanted to gain the benefits of membership whilst seeking to mitigate the (primarily political) costs. 26 of these 'yes-butters' (Äänestämme kyllä, mutta) underwrote a declaration published four days before the referendum on 12 October. One of them was Heidi Hautala who, at the Greens' party conference in June 1994, described herself as '52 per cent in favour' but told the present author on the day of the aforementioned declaration that she was a clear 'yes' at '60 per cent in favour'! The 'yes-butters' took seriously the concern of many Finns about the so-called 'democratic deficit' and, accordingly, wished to ensure that the Eduskunta (parliament) would be involved (by receiving a specific government proposal) in any decision regarding possible Finnish participation in stage three of economic and monetary union (EMU). Moreover, all decisions relating to military alignment and military action abroad were to be submitted to the people at a referendum.

Among the 'anti-marketeers', the opposition of the farmers has been noted. Their view was that the agricultural settlement was fundamentally flawed and would lead to the destruction of Finnish farming. For several public figures among the educated older generation - Jan-Magnus Jansson, a former Swedish People's Party minister, and Keijo Korhonen, a presidential candidate in January 1994 and editor of the northern newspaper

Kainuu Sanomat, for example - who were steeped in the mentality of the Cold War, the EU constituted a security risk. Membership would have deleterious implications for Russian perceptions of Finland's security and would contribute to the strategic isolation of Russia by complicating her access to the open sea. The Baltic would, in practice, become an internal EU waterway; with Russian access to the Black Sea restricted to a degree by Ukraine, the importance of the Murmansk outlet would grow. A security alignment with the West, in short, would probably lead to marked strengthening of the defence of St Petersburg and the Kola peninsula. Pursuing a NATO option would almost certainly imply concern about possible Russian aggression and send the wrong signals to Moscow. Pursuing the neutral option, however, would involve continuity in changed circumstances. Finland would seek to reforge the special relationship which was lost when the FCMA lapsed. In sum, Finland would negotiate with the Kremlin in her own name - drawing on decades of experience - rather than through the agency of the EU.

A second basic premise of the case for the neutrality option was that it would facilitate effective trade relations with eastern Europe as well as west; namely, that it would permit the economic advantages of the EEA and, in addition, the freedom to exploit the Russian and Baltic markets. The presumption here was that Russia could not be 'digested by', or fully integrated into, the EU without massive disturbance to the latter's power balance and the creation of an unwieldy internal decision-making structure. Though it may become loosely associated with the EU (itself a distant prospect), the 'widening process' would not extend to Russia which would remain an independent economic actor. As an EU member, in short, Finland would not have free hands to try and re-build its unique trade relationship with Russia.

Among the younger generations, the 'security threat' concomitant on EU membership probably carried relatively little weight. For those young people who did oppose membership, there were various explanations. Some (though by no means as many as in Sweden) occupied the high 'postmaterialist ground', questioning what the EU could do to solve the urgent global problems of poverty, pollution, disease and famine. Middle-ground opponents feared the implications of membership for the position of professional women, the welfare state and Finnish democracy. The umbrella organisation of the 'anti-marketeers', 'An Independent Finland-the Best Alternative' (Itsenäisen Suomi-Paras Vaihtoehto), stressed the loss of sovereignty and the threat membership posed to the culture of a small and relatively young nation-state; both arguments carried weight with some elements of the younger generation. Low-ground concerns ranged from the prospect of baby-food additives to the price of bananas.

It is important to stress that among a minority of persons of all ages the accession negotiations and referendum debate engendered a sense of diffuse anti-elitism and a strong reluctance to acquiesce in the 'yes' canvassed by the Establishment. There was opposition to the public posturing and disagreement between President Martti Ahtisaari and Prime Minister Esko Aho, during the summer of 1994, over whether the president or prime minister should represent Finland in the European Council and their inherent (almost pre-emptive) assumption that Finland would indeed join. There was objection too to the remnants of the 'floating log' theory - which depicted Finland floating down a river to who knows where - and particular irritation directed at a speech given by Aho on 11 October 1994 in which he claimed that observer status in the WEU would permit the nation the information and, ultimately, influence it needed. The feeling was 'why did he not say where Finland was really headed?' Some also resented as 'east European' the hob-knobby culture and special relationship cultivated by the leading Europhiles among the political elite and the inference that they had the definitive word on the subject. This 'what Delors said to me yesterday' approach could be likened, according to the anti-marketeers, to the special relationship (and, by extension, excessive power) which certain politicians enjoyed in high places in Moscow in the 1970s and early 1980s. Finally, particularly among the younger generation, there was the feeling that the referendum debate had been superficial with insufficient discussion devoted to the sort of EU Finland was proposing to join.

On 16 October 1994, 57 per cent of Finns answered in the affirmative to the question: 'Should Finland join the EU on the basis of the negotiated settlement?' Turnout, at a fraction under 74 per cent, was lower than the 83.2 per cent at the second round of presidential voting in February the same year, and lower than the 82 per cent at the Austrian EU referendum in June when over 66 per cent voted in favour. Indeed, it was comfortably the lowest of the four enlargement referenda (although higher than the only other Finnish referendum - on prohibition - in 1932) and at a separate referendum on the Åland islands on 20 November, it dropped to only 49 per cent. Most people turned out in Helsinki and its hinterland constituency Uusimaa. Approximately 1.2 million Finns cast a postal vote, compared with 1.5 million on the main polling day, Sunday 16 October, and among this group 58.9 per cent voted 'yes' and 41.9 per cent 'no'.

Table 6.1 Result of the EU referendum in Finland, October 1994

Constituency	Yes	%	No	%	Turnout
Helsinki	230,575	73.6	82,729	26.4	77.0
Uusimaa	304,778	68.0	143,126	32.0	77.0
Åland	6,041	51.9	5,608	48.1	61.0
Turku South	141,309	56.7	107,992	43.3	75.0
Turku North	76,446	50.1	76,159	49.9	74.0
Kymi	122,591	65.2	65,332	34.8	72.0
Mikkeli	59,248	54.2	49,986	45.8	68.0
Häme South	109,697	60.1	72,683	39.9	74.0
Häme North	129,568	55.6	103,263	44.4	74.0
Central Finland	66,589	47.7	72,999	52.3	72.0
Vaasa	112,586	44.4	141,236	55.6	76.0
Kuopio	65,125	48.3	69,640	51.7	68.0
Northern Karelia	43,285	48.2	46,473	51.8	66.0
Oulu	101,832	43.9	130,341	56.1	71.0
Lapland	51,871	47.4	57,476	52.6	72.0

In Finland, as in Sweden, there was a surge of support for membership in the final two weeks of the campaign. In Sweden, according to an IMU poll for Aftonbladet, there would have been a victory for the 'no' side if the referendum had been held ten days earlier. In the order of one-third of Swedes, it seems, made up their minds in the last seven days. Remarkably, an EVA poll in Finland, published on 27 September, recorded a dead-heat of 40 per cent for and against, although, significantly, in that same survey 72 per cent believed the EU supporters would come out ahead.

In Finland there was nobody with the personal stature and respect of the Norwegian prime minister Gro Harlem Brundtland or her Swedish counterpart Ingvar Carlsson backing membership, although both President Ahtisaari and former President Mauno Koivisto were vocal in their support of accession. Perhaps more significantly, there was nobody of the standing of Margareta Winberg, the Swedish Minister of Agriculture, or the Norwegian Centre Party leader, Anne Enger Lahnstein, to lead the opposition camp. True, Paavo Väyrynen, a former foreign secretary, former Centre Party chairman and former presidential candidate came down against the EU[6] but he was such a controversial character in Finland that he could well have lost the anti-marketeers in the order of 200,000 votes.

In the event, support for membership was strongest in the towns, especially in the 'deep south' and in Kauniainen it reached 87.8 per cent. In the capital city Helsinki, 73.6 per cent and 68.0 per cent in Uusimaa, voted in favour of the EU; together they virtually decided the whole result. Unlike the two other Nordic applicants, the social democratic/labour movement was solidly in favour. In Sweden, for example, an estimated 60 per cent of LO members voted against and the figures among the ruling Social Democrats, despite Carlsson's best efforts, were only 55-44 per cent in favour. In general, the 'yes' vote was greatest among the better-educated and better-off and, distinctively in the Nordic context, among young persons. This was reflected, for example, in the division in the Green Party - in contrast to Norway and Sweden where the Greens had been united in their opposition to the EU. For many Finns, including the young inter-rail generation, it appeared essentially a question of identity - a 'Yes to the West rather than Maastricht' - since many were critical of the particulars of the treaty. Closely related to the question of identity was security and, particularly among the older generation, fear of Russia and isolation ran deep. There was concern about the territorial revisionists across the eastern border - the 'Zhirinovsky factor' significantly helped the pro-EU cause - and an obvious anxiety that the alternative to EU membership was for Finland to become an islet next to Russia. Among a section of the pro-EU vote, disgruntlement with domestic politics and politicians - a diffuse politikverdrossenheit - also militated in favour of membership. The reasoning was broadly that the Brussels decision-makers must be better than the familiar faces at home.

Territorially, in the order of two-thirds of Finland (70 per cent of communes) voted 'no' and there was a majority against EU membership in the six northern constituencies - ironically those that will receive most in the way of EU support - where the (previously Agrarian) Centre Party has had its greatest strength. In Ullava, 80.6 per cent voted 'no'. From the 'No to the EU' campaign perspective, however, the turnout in the predominantly rural eastern Finland was disappointing and contributed materially to the result.   There are relatively few polling stations in the backwoods and it snowed on 16 October.   But the anti-EU campaign singularly failed to achieve the 75 per cent of Centre votes it was hoping for.   There appears to have been a conflict of loyalty among Centre voters - even in its agrarian strongholds - between allegiance to the chairman and prime minister Aho, a pro-Union man, and support for the former chairman and 'anti-marketeer', Väyrynen.

As in Norway and northern (though not southern) Sweden, the greatest opposition to the EU came from the farmers.   In February 1992, polls indicated that only 16 per cent of Finnish farmers supported an application; in November 1993, when talks appeared deadlocked, only 11 per cent favoured membership; Pesonen and Sänkiaho's eve-of-referendum survey data, moreover, show that ultimately in the order of two-thirds of the farmer-based Centre voted to stay out.[7]   In contrast to Sweden, the richer beet-growing and wheat-producing farmers of the Skåne region (the Malmöhus and Kristianstad counties) in the south, along with the agricultural producers' organisation LRF, favoured EU membership whereas in the outlying Norrland (incorporating the counties of Västernorrland, Jämtland, Västerbotten and Norrbotten) the farmers were solidly opposed.   Skåne, a region of 1.5 million persons, boasts an historic identity: about one million speak the regional dialect - since it formed part of Denmark for over eight hundred years this closely resembles Danish, but shares words in common with Icelandic - and Skåne has its own flag, which is reputedly the oldest in the Nordic states.   Yet it was less a sense of regional identity than a realisation that agricultural subsidies would rise within the EU that inclined the Skåne farmers to favour accession.   In the mostly highly-supported holdings in the far north, however, the level of subsidisation would drop.   The regional division in the attitudes of Swedish farmers to the EU is not easy to document statistically.   True, in 1994 the SOM (postal questionnaire) survey showed 75 per cent of Skåne farmers in favour and 67 per cent of those in Norrland against, but the number of farmer respondents was relatively low when the data were broken down by region.   However, when the 1991-94 SOM studies are combined, it is evident that whilst only 23 per cent of Skåne farmers were opposed to the EU, no less than 73 per cent in Norrland were against and the other 27 per cent undecided.[8]

In addition to the farmers, opposition in Finland came from the less well-off and generally from those who were pessimistic about their own economic position, especially inside the EU.   Other 'no' voters were worried about the loss of independence, a significant factor in a relatively young state such as Finland. There were relatively few 'post-materialists' among opponents of the EU, viz those who believed the EU could and would do nothing to solve wider global problems of poverty and pollution and to soften a Finnish society that had become harder and more materialist. As on the 'yes' side there were those who simply mistrusted the Helsinki elite. Where the 'No to the EU' campaign failed was in its attempt to target late middle-aged Social Democrats and ultimately to persuade sufficient women (throughout less enthusiastic than men) to come down against membership.

Finland and agriculture

The Finnish negotiators were confronted with the very difficult task of seeking to accommodate the distinctive needs of Finnish agriculture within the straightjacket of the EU's Common Agricultural Policy (CAP). Whilst geography has dealt Finnish farming a difficult hand - agricultural productivity has been low as a result of inclement climatic conditions - history, in the shape of two major land reform programmes, has compounded matters by being party, so to speak, to the creation of a preponderance of small, uneconomic, family-sized landholdings. On the latter point and paralleling similar programmes in other successor states - Czechoslovakia and Estonia, for instance - a land reform programme spanning the first decade of independence in the 1920s was conceived as a measure of social engineering and sought to consolidate bourgeois democracy against the menace of socialism and the Reds who had been defeated in the 1918 civil war. In this it was undoubtedly successful. In the first elections conducted under mass democracy in 1907, the landless rural population drew a 'red line' (punainen viiva) on their ballot papers to transform the Finnish Social Democratic Party at a stroke into the largest parliamentary party of its kind in Europe. However, profiting from the support of the newly-independent small farmers, the Agrarian Party had become the largest parliamentary party by 1929. It became a national party extending from its original strongholds in the north-west (Oulu and Vaasa) and south-east (Karelia).

Two defeats by the Soviet Union in 1939-40 (the Winter War) and 1941-4 (the so-called Continuation War) prompted an exodus of Karelian refugees who in the late 1940s were resettled on family holdings in the Finnish interior on land appropriated from the larger farmers. Virtually whole villages were relocated. Whilst the only expedient at the time, it is possible to argue that the Karelian resettlement programme both reduced the average size of farms and retarded the rapid structural development and rationalisation of agriculture which began immediately after the war in other west European countries. In Finland, it was the late 1960s before the number of farms began decreasing. Then, the rapid expansion of the manufacturing and service sectors greatly increased the demand for labour in the towns whilst new methods of farm production reduced the demand for agricultural labour. Significantly, the drift from the land involved mainly young persons and principally affected northern and eastern Finland. Many sought their fame and fortune in Helsinki; many others tried their luck in Sweden where they swelled the ranks of the factory workforce.

Since the 1960s, the acceleration of history has been remarkable and the pace of socio-economic change has been such that Finland progressed from a predominantly agricultural to a post-industrial society in the lifetime of the Winter War generation. True, 7 per cent of the economically active population engaged in agriculture in 1994 may be high compared with elsewhere in western Europe, but it is low compared with the 41.4 per cent of the Finnish population employed in agriculture and forestry in 1950. At the time of the EU application the landholding position may be summarised as follows. There were about 200,000 farms in Finland, although only about 126,000 were in active production. The average size of all farms was about 13 hectares of arable. In addition, farms had about 35 hectares of forest land. The drift from the land had led to an ageing of the agricultural population. More than two-fifths of farms were owned by farmers over 55 years. This process of senescence has been true of Norwegian farmers too. Nowadays, a minority of farmers are full-time. Only 42 per cent are engaged in full-time farming, and agriculture provides only about half the income of farm families. The most important subsidiary activities are forestry, fur-farming and horticulture.

History aside, geography has been less than kind to Finnish agriculture. The second most northerly country in the world behind Iceland (situated between the 60-70 latitudes), the growing season in Finland is short and temperatures are lower than in the EU countries. The number of days with a day/night average of +5 degrees ranges from 180 on the southern coast to 130 in Lapland, although it is true that the daily growing time in Lapland is longer in the summer since radiation lasts nearly the whole day. However, in comparison with the paucity of growing days in Finland, there are 210 in Skåne in southern Sweden which, as mentioned, was one of the most ardent pro-EU areas. In Lapland, only a few crops like hay and potatoes can be grown and important feed crops like maize and alfafa cannot be grown anywhere in Finland. The soil, moreover, is generally poor with the consequence that it is impossible to use high-yield crop varieties. This has meant that yields in Finland have been about 40-50 per cent lower than in EU countries. The non-viability of high-yield crops has raised production costs in plant production and this in turn has increased feed costs in animal production to well above the EU level. All in all, producer prices are about 30 per cent higher in Finland than Denmark.

Summing up, plant production has been concentrated in south-west Finland and grass growing in the north and east. The most common crops are barley, oats, dry hay and silage which cover 60-70 per cent of cultivated land. Wheat and rye are cultivated to meet domestic demand. Animal production (dairying) is the main output in Finland. Milk makes up about one-third of the total value of agricultural production; beef 16 per cent; and crop production about 15 per cent of total production (mainly feed grains like barley and oats).

If geography and history have dealt Finnish agriculture some indifferent cards, it has had a trump in the party political arena, in that a distinctive feature of Finland and the other two Nordic applicants has been the existence of class-specific farmers' parties, nowadays renamed Centre parties. At the time of the EU entry negotiations, the Finnish Centre was the largest single party and leading governing party with virtually 25 per cent of the vote. Exceptionally after the 1993 general election in Norway, the Centre Party, led by the fervently anti-unionist Anne Enger Lahnstein, was the second largest party in the Storting. Unlike the Norwegian party, however, the Finnish Centre has been the 'hinge group' of governing coalitions and has been consigned to opposition only twice since the Second World War - between 1987-91 and from the March 1995 general election onwards.[9]

Complementing and supplementing the Centre has been the MTK which has boasted nearly three-quarters of farmers as members. MTK consistently opposed EU membership, and eyebrows were raised when its chairman Heikki Haavisto was appointed foreign secretary of a pro-membership government in spring 1993.[10] The existence of a powerful and cohesive farm lobby, pivoting on an agrarian-Centre-MTK axis, ensured that the main goals of agricultural policy in Finland survived the transition to a service-based economy; and, until the EU application in March 1992, these basic objectives were not publicly challenged, even by the Social Democrats. The three central goals of agricultural policy - that is, the fundamental reasons for protecting agriculture - have been as follows.

First, there has been concern to achieve full self-sufficiency in foodstuffs. This has been a paramount objective, partly because much greater effort has been needed to achieve it compared with countries enjoying more conducive natural conditions. Partly too, self-sufficiency has been a concomitant of neutrality in the sense that in a crisis Finland would not have political or military allies to turn to for food supplies. The notion of economic security, alongside military security, has been common in varying degrees to all three Nordic applicant states.

Second, the aim has been to achieve an income for farmers comparable to those in other sectors of the economy, since only the larger farmers have attained something approaching parity. Indeed, the average skilled industrial worker in 1994 received a wage which was significantly higher than the per capita income of farmers. The goal of income parity has been anchored in the belief that family farms provide a stable supply of foodstuffs without being unduly susceptible to market fluctuations as well as constituting a generally stabilising force in society.

A third goal of agricultural policy has been the maintenance of a rural population. The aim has been to ensure the utilisation of resources across a country of long distances and sparse population and in so doing provide a modicum of border protection. It has in short been part of a security strategy of preserving habitation in remote areas. Norway's subsidies to farmers - at 80 per cent of the total value of agricultural output, one of the highest levels in the world - have also been designed to preserve a rural society albeit, as a NATO member, for slightly differing reasons. The public sector is more developed, and living standards are higher in rural districts than in the cities, not least because, according to the Labour Party leader, Thorbjörn Jagland, it would be considerably more expensive if people moved to the towns and the government had to deal with the accompanying social problems.[11] Incidentally, in sparsely-populated northern Norway, 70 per cent voted against EU membership in November 1994.

Far more than in the 12 existing EU member-countries, agriculture in the Nordic applicant states has been closely linked to regional, social and environmental policy. Thus, when in his opening statement at the beginning of negotiations, the Swedish foreign secretary, Ulf Dinkelspiel, referred to the Saami Lapps' right to raise reindeer, it was clear that he was less concerned with the protection of traditional nomadic lifestyles per se than the preservation of habitation in the peripheral north, namely, the utilisation of resources across the entire national territory as part of a long-pursued regional policy.

The means of achieving the three aforementioned agricultural policy goals were essentially the same in Finland, Norway and Sweden. In Finland, there was a twin strategy of price and income support (producer prices were fixed between the government and MTK) together with variable import levies and import licensing. The result was a price and sales guarantee for the entire national agricultural output regardless of domestic consumption levels. This resulted in oversupply and export subsidies in much the same way as in the EU. The main problem for Finland in contemplating the accession negotiations was that agricultural price levels and costs of production were almost twice as high as in the EU. Significantly, producer prices were approximately 30 per cent higher in Finland than in Denmark from where competition was clearly going to be the most intense.

Summing up, agriculture in the Nordic applicant states - as in many west European countries - had been a closed and subsidised sector; although all three had been wealthy enough to maintain highly protected farms characterised by low productivity and low cost efficiency. The impact of recession in Sweden and Finland, the May 1992 reforms to the EU's CAP and the December 1993 GATT agreement to cut subsidised exports combined to prompt a reappraisal of agricultural policy in the region. Sweden was first off the mark. Already in July 1991, reforms were mooted which were designed to make production more market-oriented and eradicate agricultural surpluses. The idea promoted by the Social Democratic minister of agriculture, Mats Hellström, albeit aborted in some measure by the advent of a bourgeois coalition in autumn 1991, was to abandon market and price regulation schemes and bring producer prices down to close to world market levels by 1994.

During tortuous and protracted agricultural negotiations, the Finnish EU negotiators in Brussels made two main demands. First, they argued for permanent support for what they dubbed 'Arctic farming' - that is, agriculture north of the sixtieth latitude - to accommodate the late arrival of Spring, the risky harvesting period (the bulk of the precipitation is concentrated in autumn), the relatively small scale of the active farms and the impossibility of sowing higher-yield crop varieties. Second, they argued that Finnish agriculture would not be able to withstand the absence of the type of transitional period granted to the 'convergence countries' of Spain, Portugal and Greece. Accordingly, Finland sought a twelve-year transitional period so as to implement the necessary structural improvements in agriculture. Furthermore, Finland, it was insisted, should be allowed to grant national transport subsidies for milk, meat and eggs from farms to the first point of processing/collection in support zones other than southern Finland, and also the transportation of feed to the farms in the three northern support zones where infrastructural costs were high. Other bargaining positions included quotas for milk and beet sugar; a base area for cereals and oilseeds; reference quantities for male bovine animals and suckler cow premiums; and permanent support for horticulture and seed production, since it was held that seed for Finnish climatic conditions was not available elsewhere.

The government's EU cabinet committee approved the Finnish negotiating position on agriculture on 25 August 1993, but by late November that year it became clear that there was deadlock in Brussels. Differences relating to the food sector threatened to stymie agreement on the main lines of the whole EU deal and when a settlement emerged, following a flurry of activity on 1 March 1994, it was evident that Finland had been obliged to make significant concessions. It failed to gain a transitional period for agriculture and was required to shift to EU producer prices directly on becoming a member. It did not succeed either in winning agreement on an 'Arctic farming' subsidy covering the whole country and financed conjointly with the EU. Finland would, however, receive directly from the EU in the order of two billion Finnmarks in connection with adjustments to the reformed CAP. Moreover, 85 per cent of Finnish arable and pasture land would receive subsidies under the EU's 'Less Favoured Areas' (LFA) scheme. North of the sixty-second parallel, this would take the (anomalous) form of 'mountain region' support (there are no mountains!), with the five regional sub-divisions receiving differential aid levels. South of the sixty-second latitude, it would be in the form of ordinary LFT support. The LFA subsidy, which was to cover a five-year transitional period, would not, however, embrace the wheat-producing areas of south-west Finland. Finally, drawn from the EU's structural funds, but largely benefiting agriculture, regional support was to be paid to five sparsely-populated provinces in northern and eastern Finland - Lapland, Kuusamo, Kainuu, Northern Karelia and Southern Savo - with less than eight persons per square kilometre. Covering the period 1995-9 and applying to about 16.6 per cent of the Finnish population, this new Objective Six support was created specifically to meet the special conditions of the Nordic applicant states and corresponds to Objective One funding for the poorest EU regions. Five per cent of the Swedish population qualified for Objective Six support. In addition to the above, oats were included in the EU's export subsidy scheme and quotas (albeit lower than those Finland had sought) were agreed for suger beet and milk.

Finland did manage to get the EU to accede (it was by no means automatic) to the principle of the payment of national subsidies to agriculture.   In addition to a number of short-term (essentially price-support) arrangements, two long-term measures were approved. The one related to support for those areas experiencing 'acute difficulties' which was to be negotiated in 1996 and incorporated into the Finnish budget for the following year (it might be used to compensate those south-western areas not covered by other subsidy arrangements).   The other national support measure - so-called 'northern support' (pohjoinen tuki) - was to be available on a zonal basis north of the sixty-second latitude where it was to be tied to land area and/or the number of animals.   There were, however, to be fixed production ceilings and this 'northern support' was not permitted to distort competition. On 11 September 1994, Finland won EU approval for an increase in the area covered by 'northern support': 56 per cent of its agricultural land became eligible for this national subsidy which now dipped below the sixty-second parallel to Kotka in the south-east and Taivassalo in the south-west.

At the time of the EU referendum in Finland, the possibility of EU support to 'environmentally-friendly agriculture' - principally, it was indicated, to compensate those south-western districts lacking any subsidies - was in the early stages of investigation. It was also made clear that, in a formal sense, EU approval of national support to agriculture could only be confirmed in the Commission and Council in January 1995 when and if Finland became an EU member.

The future of Finnish agriculture

Entry into the EU on 1 January 1995 was followed in short order by the election of a new government - a government far less friendly towards farming than the outgoing Centre-led Aho cabinet. Indeed, the avowed aim of the so-called 'rainbow coalition' (Social Democrats, Leftist Alliance, Swedish People's Party, Greens and Conservatives) led by the Social Democrat Paavo Lipponen, which came to power after the March 1995 general election, was to rationalise the primary sector in order to ensure its future viability.   Hence, in the 1996 budget the subsidies contained in a controversial agricultural support package steamrollered through parliament in summer 1994 were significantly reduced and, according to the new minister of agriculture, Kalevi Hemilä, a self-styled 'independent right-winger' close to the Conservatives, the objective of future subsidies would be to support those farmers (and encourage a younger generation in particular) expecting to be operating into the new millennium. His plan was to reduce the existing 115,000 holdings to 50,000 over the next 10 years. All this met with a hostile reception from the farmers. Relations with the minister deteriorated further when a 'crisis meeting' of Finnish egg producers was organised in Somero in the south-west of the country in July 1995. This underscored the problems of adjusting to EU membership - in this case the problem of a massive overproduction of eggs dating back to the 1970s - and the sharp drop in producer prices following the end of domestic protection. The mass protest was greeted by an article in the newspaper Kotimaa in which Hemilä insisted that the Finnish farmers had 'simply closed their eyes to reality'.[12] So what sort of future reality does Finnish agriculture have?

First, any analysis must be dynamic, set in the wider global environment, and take into account year-on-year variations in production, together with the likelihood of the EU widening to incorporate post-communist states by the new millennium. On the first point, the dramatic drop in EU food surpluses warrants emphasis. In 1993, there were 32 million tonnes of grain in store; by 1995, largely as a result of drought conditions, this had plummeted to 5.5 million. The EU has been obliged to return land to the plough: in 1996 farmers will be required only to keep 10 per cent of their arable fallow compared with 15 per cent in 1994. Clearly, moreover, there is great potential for increasing crop yields in eastern Europe and the former Soviet Union.[13] The implications of future EU enlargement aside, it was obvious that with producer prices determined by internal EU markets and as much as 40 per cent higher in Finland than in the EU, declining agricultural profitability would be inevitable consequence of EU accession. Hemilä's rationalisation programme is clearly a pre-requisite of the survival of an agricultural sector, not least because transitional EU support funding (LFA and Objective Six subsidies) has been agreed only to 1999. Whilst the future for Finnish farming can scarcely be described as bright, several factors could, however, combine to secure a modicum of domestic competitiveness for the agro-food sector.

First and foremost, there is its reputation for high-quality products. Thus an advantage of cold winters is that they restrict plant disease and the insect population and so minimize the use of pesticides. The use of fertilisers has also been lower in Finland than in other EU countries since the poor quality of the soil imposes natural limits to the extent of the value-added to be gained from fertilisation, twice as much is clearly not twice as good. Low population and traffic density have spared plants the worst effects of lead and cadmium pollution and the very high hygiene standards in the slaughterhouses have meant the absence of a salmonella risk. It is worth noting too that transportation costs constitute a natural barrier which might help to maintain slightly higher price levels in Finland compared with the average EU price level. Furthermore, despite strong EU competition, particularly from the Danes, Finnish agriculture may be able to secure niche export markets. Already, Finnish pork and ham are exported from a pig farm in Karkkila to Paris whilst the firm Arctic Taste in Janakkala delivers caraway seeds without an export subsidy to the EU spice centres of Rotterdam and Hamburg. Aromatic plants, cultivated on fallow, are particularly suited to Finland because of the light summer period. There may also be potential for the export of reindeer meat since EU membership has provided protection against the Russian reindeer trade.

Undue optimism should none the less be avoided. The greatest problem of adjustment will be in the area of crop production - Sweden in contrast has much better crop competitiveness - and only the largest and most efficient grain farms look likely to survive. Finland's best prospects would appear to lie in the field of beef and dairy farming - where the price differential with the EU is smallest - along with a general diversification of production. A model of economically and ecologically sustainable dairy farming - dairying is presently spread throughout Finland - would place the emphasis on the quality of production and preserve, in accordance with the prerequisites of national economic security, farming activity in the country's border regions. Ironically, the emotive slogan used by a rally of four thousand farmers from MTK's six southern regions on 29 November 1993 - 'Inside the EU Finland will become simply a reindeer farming area' did not completely miss the mark. Future EU support will very probably be for precisely the type of specialist (niche) production of the likes of reindeer farming.

Notes

1.   Max Jakobson.

2.   Arter, David., *Politics and Policy-Making in Finland*, Wheatsheaf, Brighton, 1987, pp. 176-95. For new evidence on the 'Note Crisis' see 'Sotilaitten Nootti', *Helsingin Sanomat*, 29 October 1995.

3.   Allison, Roy, *Finland's Relations with the Soviet Union: 1944-84*, MacMillan, London, 1985, pp. 95-8. See also Arter, David, *The Politics of European Integration in the Twentieth Century*, Dartmouth, Aldershot, 1993.

4.   Rehn, Olli, 'Odottavasta ennekoivaan integraatiopolitiikaan?', in *Johdatus Suomen Ulkopolitiikaan*, Tuomas Forsberg and Tapani Vaahtoranta (eds), Gaudeamus, Tampere, 1993, pp. 188-9.

5.   Arter, David, 'The EU Referendum in Finland on 16 October 1994: A Vote for the West, not for Maastricht', *Journal of Common Market Studies*, vol. 33, no. 3, 1995, pp. 361-87.

6.   Väyrynen, Paavo, 'Europeisk union eller Nordisk gemenskap?', *Nordisk Kontakt*, no. 9, 1994, pp. 4-11.

7.   Pesonen, Pertti and Sänkiaho, Risto, 'The Finnish Referendum on Membership in the EU', in *Yearbook of Finnish Foreign Policy*, Finnish Institute of International Affairs, Forssa, 1994, p. 55.

8.   'EU kaksinkertaistaisi Ruotsin maataloustuen', *Helsingin Sanomat*, 12 November 1994; 'Skoonelaisviljelijä rikastuisi entisestään EU-Ruotissa', *Helsingin Sanomat*, 12 November 1994; Ruotsin "kyllä" EU: lle kytkisi skoonen Tanskaan', *Helsingin Sanomat*, 10 November 1994.

9.   Arter, David, 'The Finnish Centre Party: Profile of a "Hinge Group"', *West European Politics*, vol. 2, no. 1, 1979, pp. 108-27.

10. For a discussion of MTK's changed role since Finland joined the EU, see 'MTK: n menetetty mahti' ja 'EU vie maatalousvallen ministeriöltä', *Helsingin Sanomat*, 13 August 1995.

11. 'Öljytalous Kannattelee Norjaa', *Helsingin Sanomat*, 4 September 1995; 'Into Europe', *The Economist*, 5 November 1994, pp. 20-2.

12. 'Rakennemuutos aiheuttaa kipuja maataloudessa', Helsingin Sanomat, 26 July 1995.

13. 'The food runs out', *Independent on Sunday*, 12 November 1995.

7 Norway: the One that got away

CLIVE ARCHER[1]

Introduction

In September 1972, the Norwegian electorate rejected the terms of entry into the then European Communities (EC) negotiated by its minority Labour government. In November 1994, Norwegians again threw out the terms of membership - this time of the European Union (EU) - agreed by a minority Labour government. Of the four applicants in 1972, Norway was the only one to say 'no' and, likewise, Norway was the lone recalcitrant of the quartet of applicants in 1994.

This chapter will examine the background to the Norwegian application, the negotiations with the EU, the main aspects of the referendum campaign, the outcome of the referendum, and the situation thereafter. It will particularly look more closely at two particular issues that were of importance to Norway in the negotiations, the energy sector and fisheries, and will refer to those issues in the negotiations of the other applicants.

Norway applied for EU membership in November 1992. Though Norwegian access to the EU's Single Market had been largely secured with the European Economic Area (EEA) agreement, the Labour government feared that a further extension to include other EFTA members would work to Norway's detriment unless it also became a full member. The government feared that the country would become more marginalised politically, and in the security field, in post-Cold War Europe. Norway's traditionally strong link with NATO (North Atlantic Treaty Organisation) did not seem to hold the promise it had previously because of the weakened position of the United States (US) in Europe. Prospective Norwegian associate membership of the Western European Union (WEU) provided only limited access to the institutions' decision-making process, but full EU membership, with participation in its Common Foreign and Security Policy (CFSP), was seen as providing Norway with greater access to European security decision-making at a time when Norway had an uncertain neighbour to the north and east, Russia.

Norway opened its negotiations with the European Communities for EU membership on 5 April 1993, two months after Austria, Finland and Sweden. The Norwegian application for accession did not raise any political problems as Norway fulfilled the three major EU membership preconditions (European identity, democracy, and upholding human rights), was a founder member of NATO and was an associate of the WEU. Norway already had a free trade arrangement with the EU and had ratified the EEA agreement between the EU and other EFTA states. By signing the EEA agreement, Norway had taken on the *acquis communautaire* - the EU's backlog of primary and secondary legislation - related to the free movement of capital, labour, goods and services. In applying for EU membership, Norway had to accept that no permanent derogations, only transitional arrangements, could be given for problem sectors.[2] From the beginning, problems arising from Norwegian membership were identified from the EU side, especially in energy, fisheries, agriculture, regional policy, state aid and state monopolies, alcohol restrictions, social policy and trade policy.[3]

The historical background

Norway had been a founder member of EFTA in 1960 when the organisation had been established as a free trade alternative to the then European Economic Community. However, Norwegian membership of EFTA was undertaken more because the other Nordic states and the United Kingdom (UK) would be members than for positive reasons. After all, EFTA aimed at free trade in industrial goods rather than farming and fisheries products, in which Norway had an interest.

Norway had submitted its first application for EU membership in May 1962 after the UK and Denmark had applied in July 1961, but this fell with de Gaulle's veto on British membership in January 1962. Another French veto, in July 1967, led to proposals for closer Nordic economic cooperation (Nordek), which were suspended in March 1970.[4] After the December 1969 Hague Summit, the EU re-opened negotiations with the UK, Denmark, Norway and Ireland and the four accession treaties were signed in January 1972. A new national campaign was established in August 1970 with the title of the 'People's Movement against Norwegian membership of the Common Market'. Representatives from groups opposing membership and all the political parties' youth organisations, were included.[5] In its report on Norwegian EU membership, the People's

Movement criticised the Rome Treaty for its free-market approach, and warned that Norwegian EU membership would take away political control over the economy and would lead to social injustice.[6]

In March 1971, the centre-right coalition,[7] which had been divided over the EU, resigned, making way for a minority Labour government that was prepared to push ahead with membership. Indeed, in August 1972, the Labour government announced that it would resign in the case of a 'no' vote in the referendum.

Norwegian membership was rejected by 53.5 per cent against 46.5 per cent of those voting in a politically divisive referendum in September 1972. The referendum result led to the fall of the Labour government, and a deep rift within Norwegian politics and society. It divided not only the political parties, but town and countryside; two divisions re-emerged, one along a territorial centre-periphery divide and one on an urban-rural axis.[8] Support for membership increased with urbanisation and in densely populated areas, while it decreased in smaller and sparsely populated communities and in those dependent on the primary sector. The agricultural and the fisheries sectors showed that they still had political strength and - when joined with the radical urban intellectuals - could veto EU membership.

After the failure to take up full EU membership from 1 January 1973, an industrial free trade area was negotiated between Norway and the Communities. The issue of full membership was taken off the political agenda in Norway for the rest of the 1970s and the early 1980s. By 1984, the EU had started plans for a Single European Market (SEM) by 1992 and, in response, the EFTA states, including Norway, advanced the idea of a closer EFTA-EU link. By 1989 this proposal had matured into plans for an EEA between EFTA and the EU.

The EEA agreement offered Norwegian industry access to the EU's internal market. While Austria wished to apply for full EU membership, the other EFTA states - including Norway - had reservations.[9] In Norway, the coalition government's inaugural statement ruled out a customs union and the free movement of persons between the EU and EFTA,[10] but this approach was altered in December 1989 - probably in response to fast-moving events in Europe - to one of keeping the customs union option open.[11]

In November 1990, a new minority Labour government came to power but did not officially tackle the EU issue until late 1991, after the government had agreed to the terms of the EEA Treaty. It was originally hoped that the EEA - which was expected to start on 1 January 1993 -

would help ease Norway into the EU for, say 1996, by making the Norwegian public used to the new aspects of the SEM.[12] However, this timetable had to be altered after the Swedish Social Democratic government decided to apply for membership in July 1991, and was followed by Finland. This meant that Norway's neutral Nordic neighbours had taken the lead, and the delay of the start of the EEA until 1 January 1994 further challenged Norwegian government plans. As the security aspect of the EU was to be discussed at an intergovernmental conference (IGC) in 1996 and as this was seen as an important aspect of Norway's relations with the EU,[13] then it seemed logical that Norway should join by 1996. Norway's application was submitted in November 1992, after EEA legislation had been accepted. This allowed Norway to be included with the other three EFTA applicants. Ironically, by the time Norway had applied for EU membership, the initial enthusiasm about the Union had disappeared and had been replaced by Euro-scepticism, even within the core states of the organization.

The Norwegian Labour government had to overcome three obstacles before achieving the goal of EU membership: negotiations with the EU; the referendum campaign; and opposition in parliament. It successfully undertook the first but then stumbled and fell at the second.

Membership negotiations

During the 1970-2 application, negotiations with the EU proved to be important for three reasons. First, they delayed the 'Yes' campaign in Norway from properly starting its offensive until the outcome of the negotiations were known, whereas the 'No' campaign was not so constrained. Secondly, it was recognised that the outcome of the fisheries agreement was one that was unacceptable to Norwegian fishermen, and, indeed, the Minister of Fisheries resigned in protest at the deal. Thirdly, although energy was not then a subject for the membership negotiations, a remark by a member of the Commission staff that the newly-developed Norwegian offshore energy resources would become a Community resource, cost the pro-membership cause a number of votes.

The 1993-4 negotiations were completed relatively quickly but still the 'No' campaign had the advantage that, unlike the membership supporters, it did not have to wait for the final outcome before launching its campaign. Secondly, fisheries and petroleum proved again to be two key areas, joined by agriculture and regional policy. There was, as in 1972, the broader sovereignty issue, which proved to be of major importance to Norwegian domestic opinion. In the case of fisheries and energy, the EU was changing its own policies, making these highly salient matters in the accession negotiations.

Norway, like the other applicant countries, had to accept the *acquis communautaire* in full, but much of this had already been adopted during the EEA negotiations. As in 1971, any adjustment had to be made through transitional arrangements. The two main themes of fisheries and energy will now be examined in more detail, with particular reference to the Norwegian negotiations. Although the three other applicant countries had interests in these areas, none of them had such an important stake in either question as Norway.

Fisheries

In 1992, fish was the third most important of Norway's mainland exports with 90 per cent of the total catch exported, 67 per cent to the EU,[14] of whose fish imports Norway supplied a quarter.[15] The Norwegian fisheries minister, Jan Henry T. Olsen, declared at the start of the negotiations that Norway had no fish to give away[16] and he requested adjustments to the Common Fisheries Policy (CFP).[17]

Partly because of the negative experience with the issue in 1972, the minority Labour administration showed caution over fisheries in the 1993-4 negotiations. It wished to see the principle of 'relative stability' continue as the basis for the distribution of quotas.[18] Norway wanted to keep its then current quotas with other states, and to uphold its strict enforcement of quotas and catching regulations. It also wanted complete free access to the EU for its fisheries products which had been partly achieved within the EEA. Norway requested that the link between the survival of its coastal settlements and the fish resources on which they depended to be recognised, and wanted the 12 mile exclusive fisheries zone to be maintained at least until 2002. It also wished to keep its system of direct sales associations. In the light of the range and importance of its fishing industry, Norway considered that it should play a major role in the development of the EU's new CFP and that Norway's interests should be reflected therein.[19]

Many of Norway's negotiating points were contested both by the EU Commission and by certain EU members, most noticeably France and Spain, with some support from the UK. The French government, faced with pressure from its own fishermen in early 1994, tried to exclude Norwegian fish imported under the EEA arrangements.[20]   The Spanish government demanded that an additional annual quota of 11,000 tonnes of cod from Norwegian waters should be allowed for the southern EU members, with 7,000 tonnes going to Spain.[21]   The Commission rejected Norway's request to 'retain sole control over resources north of 62 degrees latitude' which include the sensitive Russian-Norwegian 'Grey Zone'.[22] This is the offshore area in the Barents Sea disputed between the two countries.   The two have agreed an annual total catch in part of the area and the division of the catch between Norway, Russia and third states.[23]

When most Norwegian-EU negotiations ended in March 1994, the deal obtained by Norway on fisheries appeared to be better than that of 1972. On the one hand, the Commission could not accept demands for market access without reciprocity, but, as Norwegian membership would increase the tonnage of the EU's fishing fleet by 17 per cent,[24] the Commission was prepared to compromise on a number of issues.

The Norwegian fisheries Minister was able to find fish to exchange, if not give away, and under the EEA settlement Norway had already agreed to a gradual increase in EU fishing quotas for Norwegian Arctic cod.[25]   In the end, the fisheries Minister, Jan Henry T. Olsen, felt able to recommend the agreement, unlike his predecessor in 1972.

Norway was to have duty-free access for its seafood to EU markets from the first day of membership, though the sales of eight species (such as salmon) - should these cause serious market disturbances - could be limited by the EU in a transitional period of four years.   These were species where there was competition with existing EU states.   Norway was to retain its 12-nautical mile exclusive coastal fishing zone, and the interests of coastal communities should be stressed when the zone's continuation was to be discussed in 2002.   Furthermore, the EU accepted that a future permanent system of fish quotas was to be based on the principle of 'relative stability' as urged by Norway.

More controversial was the complicated agreement for EU cod quotas in the seas north of 62 degrees north.   The Norwegian government accepted that there had been a concession to the EU of 2,000 tonnes of cod beyond the quotas agreed in the EEA treaty.   However, the estimation of the main Norwegian fishermen's organization was that 20,000 tonnes of cod had been ceded.[26]   The right of management of the waters north of 62 degrees was to be transferred to the EU no later than 1 July 1998.   Also from that date; the EU would take over Norway's annual negotiations with Russia regarding the management of the 'grey zone' in the Barents Sea.   In addition, the EU would take over management of fish resources in Norwegian waters south of 62 degrees latitude from the first day of membership.

Another contentious point was the retention for a transitional period of three and a half years only of the Norwegian laws requiring Norwegian citizenship for the ownership of Norwegian registered fishing vessels, after which EU citizens would be able to buy Norwegian boats. Furthermore, EU market regulations for the sale of fish would replace Norwegian ones, and membership of the wholesalers' cooperative would no longer be compulsory.[27] Norwegian negotiators had decided to exchange ultimate control over its offshore fisheries - plus some tonnes of cod - for greater access to the EU's lucrative market.

The fishermen's organisations rejected such a deal and condemned the negotiated terms.[28] The concessions to Spain were an irritant, but their central point was that Norway would lose the right and the ability to regulate fishing in what they regarded as Norwegian waters. They had had a clientele relationship with the government in Oslo whereby the two sides - fishermen and government - dealt directly with each other over a range of issues. They were not prepared to give this up and become only one group among a number that would have an input into EU decision-making on fisheries matters.

Off-shore petroleum

When membership of the EU was being debated by Norwegians in 1972, oil and gas had been discovered offshore but the country was only at the start of an era in which it became a major oil state. However, it was clear that oil and gas could make a major contribution to the Norwegian economy and to the wealth of the Norwegian people. The Norwegian public thus responded with shock and disapproval when, some days before the EU membership referendum, a leaked memorandum from a Commission official referred to Norway's oil being a 'Community resource' once Norway had joined the EU.[29] This unwise statement clearly cost the pro-EU campaign votes.

During the 1993-4 round of negotiations, the EU advanced a draft directive that concerned the licensing of off-shore oil and gas development and would have affected Norway's resources, had it joined. The Commission advanced its draft in March 1992 (adopted in May 1994) and it propounded the idea that EU companies should be able to bid for offshore resources on a non-discriminatory basis, regardless of their nationality or whether they were state-owned or private.[30]   The draft directive would have undermined Statoil's automatic part ownership of all blocks on the Norwegian Continental shelf and its position as both operator and administrator of the State's Direct Economic Engagement in off-shore activity.[31]   However, the new draft directive confirmed for the first time that off-shore resources belonged to the state in whose sector they were found, and were national, rather than EU resources.[32]   The mistake of September 1972 was not to be repeated.

One answer to the question of Statoil's status would have been to separate the State's Direct Economic Engagement off-shore from Statoil and to hand it to the Norwegian Ministry of Industry and Energy, thus allowing Statoil to act as a normal competitive company.[33]   This would have curtailed Statoil's lead position in Norway's Gas Negotiating Committee (GFU), the membership of which had already been broadened.[34]   A number of other Norwegian companies favoured this solution.[35]   However, Statoil has been an important instrument by which the Norwegian government can control the utilisation of its off-shore resources. By 1993, Norway was challenging the UK as the main oil producer in the North Sea and an important section of its economy was dependent on oil and gas. The Norwegian government neither wished to rush into a change of the conditions for off-shore production, nor wanted to be seen to alter its resources policy to come into line with EU policy which Norway had not helped to formulate.

Such a prospect was avoided by Protocol 4 of the Accession Treaty[36] which confirmed Norwegian jurisdiction over its petroleum resources and recognised the right of state participation in the offshore sector.   The protocol reiterated national rights over the management of those resources. Protocol 4 thus defused the issue of the control of Norway's oil and gas and it then played little part in the referendum campaign.

Already existing directives - the Utilities Directive (90/531/EEC) and its subsequent Remedies Directive - could have had an equally serious direct effect on national preference in the Norwegian off-shore sector. Furthermore, the effect of these directives, intended to open up supply and other off-shore activity to EU-wide tendering, could still be extended to Norway through the EEA,[37] though with Norway having little chance to shape its implementation.

Other issues

The agreement reached between the EU and Norway covered a wide range of issues from those dealing with the CFSP to the number of Norwegian members of the European Parliament (EP). In particular two other related policy issues - agriculture and regional aid - impinged on the internal debate in Norway, and the whole question of sovereignty became vital to the wider debate between the 'yes' and 'no' sides.

Norway shared the view of Finland and Sweden that the EU should grant their agriculture a special Arctic and sub-Arctic status. The Norwegian government's case to the Commission was that the climatic, topographical and demographic conditions of their country's agriculture should be compensated by guaranteeing Norwegian producers earnings similar to those of farmers elsewhere in the EU.[38]

The settlement extended the EU's CAP to Norway, with the country adjusting to EU agricultural prices from the first day of membership, subject to special measures to prevent severe market disruption during the first five years. The CAP's support policy was to cover the whole of northern Norway and parts of the south, with the addition of national support being allowed. However, total and permanent support could not exceed the existing level and subsidies contrary to current CAP schemes were to be phased out over five years. Norway was also to have a seven-year period to subsidise farms producing pork, poultry and eggs, which otherwise did not reach EU subsidy criteria.[39]

Norwegian regional policy, like that of the EU, was aimed at avoiding depopulation of outlying regions and at bringing new development to rural areas.[40] Norway requested that all of the country from Trondheim up to the Russian border should get EU support as especially underdeveloped regions.[41]

In the March 1994 agreement, population density was used as the criterion for regional aid under new Objective 6. Norway's four northernmost counties - Finnmark, Troms, Nordland and Nord Trøndelag - would receive about Nkr0.5bn yearly from EU funds, with the Norwegian government providing matching grants.[42]

Norway's ability to make its own decisions had been a major issue in the 1972 campaign and was again taken up by anti-membership campaigners who portrayed Brussels as remote, interfering and having a different agenda from the one Norway should have.[43]

Mrs Brundtland attempted to respond by describing EU membership as 'additional democracy', giving Norway the sort of control over the international aspect of policies that it could not obtain alone. Furthermore, she suggested - without further elaboration - that 'if Norway wants to leave the EU after first having entered into it, the issue will be decided by a majority in the *Storting*'.[44] A further point was that the 25 million Nordic citizens would have a larger weighted vote in the Council - if the three Nordic applicants joined - than that of Germany with its 80 million citizens. Three votes each from Finland and Norway and four from Sweden would be added to Denmark's three, giving the Nordic bloc 13 votes in a Qualified Majority Vote, compared with Germany's ten.

Fish and energy generally

The questions of the terms of entry for Norway brought the fisheries issue to the fore, and - even though offshore petroleum did not become a major bone for contention - it had the potential to cause difficulties. Both issues turned out to be overwhelmingly of interest to Norway among the four applicant states. Clearly, fisheries was a subject of economic and political importance to the then existing members of the EU, especially the UK, Spain, France and Ireland. Of the other applicants, land-locked Austria had little direct claim on the subject. However, both Sweden and Finland had Baltic fishing interests that had to be satisfied. Compared with Norwegian concerns, these were minor matters and were settled fairly expeditiously.

Finland and Sweden were to participate in the CFP from their first day of membership, meaning that their fisheries products would be tariff-free within the EU. Structural support for the fishing industry meant that it could benefit from EU funding up to half of the amount required.[45] Furthermore, Sweden was to have a larger share of the Baltic Sea cod quota, perhaps reflecting the 125,000 sq.km of Baltic Sea that Swedish membership added to Community waters.[46] Finland was allowed a three year period to continue herring fishing in the Baltic for fishmeal purposes.[47]

None of the other three states have offshore petroleum resources of any size. Both Sweden and Finland had some interest in making sure that Norwegian resources were open to all EU members, as both countries have had some problems with energy supplies. Finland's traditional source of energy, the Soviet Union, had collapsed and supplies from Russia were uncertain. Swedish governments had promised to decommission the country's nuclear power stations, but were faced with a gap between energy demand and supply should that task be undertaken. Much of the gas from Norwegian offshore fields was to be piped to the European continent. Access to such a ready source of dependable energy was more affected by economic and physical circumstances - the cost and feasibility of directing gas to Sweden and Finland - rather than by EU policy.

The referendum campaign

The contrast between the campaigns of the two sides in the referendum resembled that seen in the 1972 campaign. By the time the government applied for membership, the 'No to the EU' movement was already organized on a nation-wide basis. The 'Yes' campaign was more fragmented, unclear about their message[48] and took longer to get started. Pro-membership groups had a number of disadvantages. First, they could not campaign in favour of the terms of membership until these had been decided, which was March 1994, with some details not being settled until weeks before the referendum. Secondly, while the 'No' groups sank their differences in a common front against the EU, the political divisions between the representatives of business - and their Conservative Party parliamentary colleagues - and the labour movement and the Labour government was deep and traditional. Finally, as in 1972, the 'No' campaign had grass-roots support - with 442 local teams and 19 larger regional divisions - while the 'Yes' supporters were more likely those with a professional interest in membership, thereby reducing the impact of their message. On the other hand, the opposition of the farmers and fishermen was shown as protecting the Norwegian way of life rather than as an expression of self-interest.

The 'No' campaign was supported financially by the farmer's organization and the fishermen. Industry backed the 'Yes' campaign, but the trade unions were reluctant to be closely involved with either side. Indeed, by September 1994, a special meeting of the LO - the Norwegian Federation of Trade Unions - decided by 156 votes to 149 to oppose membership.[49] In 1972, the LO's leadership had supported joining the EU despite opposition from most of their members.[50]

The settlement made with the EU was negotiated by Mrs Brundtland's Labour government which was reluctant to leave the outcome of the referendum to fate. The Prime Minister, in particular, had a strategy which, she hoped, would lead to Norwegian EU membership. Unfortunately for her, events did not favour her plan.

The Copenhagen European Council decided on a timetable for the admission of the EFTA applicants to the EU by 1 January 1995, but this presented problems for the Norwegian Labour government. It had been hoped that the negotiations would take time, and that this would allow the Norwegian population to be 'acclimatised' to the EU through the implementation of the EEA. They would then realise that they had accepted the SEM aspects of the EU but would want a greater say in its implementation. Lengthy negotiations would have given the government the opportunity to be seen to be standing up for Norwegian interests against the EU. Finally, it would have allowed Austria, Sweden and Finland to decide in referenda to join the EU, making it easier to persuade the Norwegian people to come in with their Nordic neighbours and EFTA colleagues.[51]

However, the Norwegian hope for a long lead-in period before full membership proved to be blighted. *At the EU level*, the Maastricht Process was slowing in 1992-93, with the Danish referendum producing a 'no' result, the French '*petit oui*' and the UK's troubled ratification process. The international economic recession and collapse of the Exchange Rate Mechanism (ERM), weakening plans for the European Monetary Union (EMU) - plus the failure of the EU in Yugoslavia - lessened the attraction of European integration for Nordic voters. Also, after the Swiss people had refused to ratify the EEA, it only started functioning from 1 January 1994, a year later than planned.

At the Nordic level, support for the EU as shown in opinion polls in Sweden and Finland declined during 1993, and the economies of the Nordic countries suffered badly.[52] This could be seen as a factor that may have made EU membership more attractive. Instead, it tended to emphasise the mood of uncertainty among the Nordic electorate.

The 1993 Norwegian general election demonstrated that the Labour and Conservative parties had been unsuccessful in silencing the membership issue. The anti-EU parties won more than one quarter of the seats in the *Storting*, with the Centre Party going up from 11 to 32 seats. The anti-EU Socialist Left Party went down four seats to 13, but together the anti-EU groups had 45 seats, more than they needed to block membership outright.[53] According to paragraph 93 of the Norwegian constitution, a three-quarter majority of the *Storting* (parliament) is needed to delegate sovereignty to an international organisation such as the EU. Even if a consultative referendum proved to be in favour of membership, the final decision had to be taken by the *Storting* where 42 representatives could thus block EU membership. Divisions within the Labour Party started to reappear once the negotiations opened. As in 1972 a Labour Party anti-EU group - Social democrats against the EU (SME) - was formed.[54] Public opinion was distinctly against joining the EU with all opinion polls during 1993 showing majorities against membership - by October 1993 51 per cent were against, with only 23 per cent in favour.[55]

The outcome

Norway held its advisory referendum on accession to the EU on 27 and 28 November 1994. There was a 88.8 per cent turnout, compared with 79.2 per cent in 1972. Of those voting, 52.3 per cent said 'no' to membership, and 47.7 per cent said 'yes'. This represented just a 0.6 per cent swing to the 'yes' side from 1972. Mrs Brundtland's government accepted the result and the accession treaty was never placed before the *Storting*.

Although about a half of 1994's voters were not franchised in 1972, the two referenda have remarkably similar profiles. In both 1972 and 1994, the countryside and the north voted 'no' and the town and the south-east (around Oslo) 'yes'. Likewise the counter-culture of primary producers and urban radicals, together with the users of New Norwegian (the minority language associated with the west coast) united against those in the capital and those in trade and commerce. Workers were more opposed to the EU than their white-collared colleagues, and the left-wing more than those on the right of the political spectrum.[56]

One of the major differences was in the turnout. In 1972 a number of Labour supporters seemed to stay at home as 'sofa voters' rather than contribute to their government's downfall by voting 'no' or go against their conscience and vote 'yes'. By 1994 the cross-pressure had eased. In the 1993 election, the Centre Party appeared to win votes by playing the anti-EU card, whereas the Labour Party kept and even increased its vote by ignoring the EU issue.[57] Labour partly had to do this as the negotiations with the EU had not finished, but the party also wanted to play down an issue that split its support. Compared with 1972, the Labour Party was relatively unscathed by its referendum 'defeat', obtaining its highest opinion poll figure since 1977 only a month after the November vote.[58]

A second difference was in the voting habits of women in 1994. In 1972 the preferences of men and women were fairly similar, but in 1994 57 per cent of women voted 'no' and 52 per cent of men voted 'yes'.[59] This can partly be explained by the growth in the number of women working in the public sector, the assumption being that they saw the EU as a threat to the welfare-state and the public-sector in Norway. Unlike 1972, some 57 per cent of those in private sector jobs voted for EU membership.[60] However, it seems that women voted more heavily against the EU more generally, not just in the public sector.[61]

The issues for discussion - fisheries, offshore oil and gas, agriculture and regional policy, and sovereignty - had been prominent in 1972. The most vocal opposition to membership came from the same quarters - the urban left and the rural voters - while a 'yes' was recommended by a Labour government and by business groups. The grass-roots 'No' movement started its campaign well before the 'Yes' organisation had an agreement to defend. Some of the labour movement were supporters of the 'No' campaign, as in 1972. Clearly in both 1972 and 1994, the issue was of high political salience, with the referendum being hotly contested.

However, there were a number of *differences* between the two campaigns. First and foremost, the international and European contexts were changed. The Cold War was over and the EC had become the EU. The Union had its CFSP with the prospect of a common defence policy. In the intervening years, the EU had developed regional, social and environmental policies that it did not have in 1972. The economies of the west European countries became more integrated in terms of trade, commerce, capital and even labour. Norway had already accepted the EEA before the 1993 negotiations, whereas the option of a free trade agreement with the EU only arose in 1973 after Norway had rejected full membership. Both the EU's agricultural and fisheries policies are to undergo major changes within the next ten years. More decisions have been taken by majority votes in the Council of Ministers, and the power of the EP has increased. By 1994 the EU contained the UK, Ireland and Denmark, as well as the Mediterranean members acquired in the 1980s. In other words, it was a different organisation from the EU in 1972 and it was set in a totally altered Europe. This meant that the 1994 membership question was not just a replay of 1972.

Secondly, there was the Nordic element. In 1972, none of the Nordic states were members of the EU and the Norwegian referendum was held a week before that of Denmark. Opponents could thus claim that all the Nordic states had the option of forming an economic bloc outside the EU. By 1994, Denmark had already been a member of the EU for over twenty years and was a founder - though somewhat reluctant - member of the EU. As the Norwegian referendum was held after those of both Finland and Sweden, it was known that both would join the EU.

Thirdly, the 1994 settlement was different from that in 1972. Account had been taken of the special conditions of Nordic agriculture, and the fisheries settlement was accepted by a self-confessed sceptical Minister. Furthermore, three of the Ministers negotiating in Brussels were former opponents of membership.

Finally, the position of the Labour government can be compared with that of the 1972 administration. Mrs Brundtland went into the negotiations with a strong political base, having been returned to power after the 1993 elections. The strengthening of anti-membership parties in that election paradoxically may have strengthened Norway's hand in Brussels and allowed its negotiators to fend off more easily Spanish demands on fishing. Key countries such as Germany and France realised that Norway had to have a satisfactory settlement if its government had any hope of winning a referendum. Also, the Labour government was aware during these negotiations of the dangers of a repeat of 1972. The original stress on the EEA; the cautious approach to application; the positioning of former opponents in negotiating roles; and the push for an 'acceptable' settlement, all suggest that Mrs Brundtland was determined not to make what were perceived as the same 'mistakes' as had Labour in 1972. Not making the question one of confidence for the Labour government meant that the 'no' vote had a limited effect on the Labour party in 1995, compared with the electoral disaster of 1973.

Aftermath

Norway had both an economic and political soft landing after the referendum. Unlike 1972, when a free trade agreement had to be negotiated with the EU by a weak minority government, the Brundtland government stayed in power in charge of a strong economy, safe in the knowledge that the EEA already provided Norway with an economic framework in its relations with the EU.

Since the 'no' vote, the growth of the Norwegian economy has slowed somewhat, but this has been more a reflection of a general economic slow-down in 1995, compared with 1994, than a reaction to the country's self-exclusion from the EU. Indeed, a number of indicators show Norway to be out-performing its EU neighbours. Growth in GDP per capita in 1994 - at 5.7 per cent - placed Norway sixth in the OECD list on that count. The first half of 1995 showed a growth of some 4 per cent compared with the same period in 1994,[62] with prognostications for the whole of 1995 suggesting that Norway will still doing better than Germany, the UK, Italy and Sweden.[63] Furthermore, Norwegian exports in the first half of 1995 showed an 8 per cent increase on the same period the year before,[64] with a merchandise trade surplus of some Nkr26.6bn ($4.2bn) being reported for the period.[65] Norway's central budget deficit has fallen dramatically in 1995, with a surplus forecast for 1996[66] and interest rates have remained stable, so that Norway has been one of the few west European states that - ironically in its case - could fulfil the convergence criteria set out in the Maastricht treaty for EMU. Employment has continued to rise in Norway, which has the lowest unemployment figure - 5.2 per cent in 1995 - in OECD-Europe.[67]

This is not to say that remaining outside the EU has been free of cost. Since the Norwegian referendum, the government has confirmed its wish to continue with the EEA and EFTA.[68] However, it has also been clear that Norway cannot 'pick and choose' from the EU menu[69] and will have to accept a number of decisions through the EEA over which it has little control. Norway has anyhow had to accept the EU's Concessions Directive on the exploration and exploitation of offshore oil, opening up commercial access to its resources to other EEA states.[70] Joint management of fish stocks in the North Sea was agreed with the EU in February 1995,[71] though a new deal on tariff-free fish exports to the three EFTA states that joined the EU was held up for some time by the Swedes,[72] and the EU was dragged into Norway's fisheries dispute with Iceland.[73] However, there has been little sign of capital flight from Norway or of major businesses relocating away from the country. Norway has been careful to associate itself with the EU's CFSP by formalising contact and dialogue with the EU in that area,[74] though it will only have an indirect input into the consideration of matters such as the future of the WEU and the defence aspect of the EU when these are considered at the 1996 IGC.

Given the good economic conditions in Norway and the relatively low perceived cost of remaining outside the EU, the Labour government has suffered little from being on the opposite side to the majority of the electorate in the referendum. This is mainly because most of the electorate has a general confidence in the government's handling of the economy, and partly because the opposition is divided and weak. The Centre Party - which seemed to be one of the main beneficiaries of the referendum result - found itself losing seats and votes in the September 1995 local elections. The Labour Party's share of the vote was down from the 1993 general election but increased from the previous local elections in 1991.[75]

The government's success with the economy has been, however, dependent on the wider world situation and, more specifically, on the world market in oil and gas. Oil and natural gas production from the Norwegian continental shelf rose between the first half of 1994 and the first half of 1995 by 4.6 per cent, making Norway the main North Sea oil producer. Gas sales to continental Europe have been agreed until well into the next century.[76] These exports have allowed Norway to maintain a buoyant economy and will allow the country to finance its welfare state at a time when its population is ageing. It seems that, with the insurance of petroleum production, Norway will suffer few immediate or long-term economic consequences of exclusion from the EU.

Conclusion

While it is tempting to see the Norwegian result as part of a wider Euro-scepticism sweeping Europe since the signing of the Maastricht Treaty, this would deny the significance of the close correlation with the 1972 result. It seems more likely that, once again, the European issue opened up old territorial and cultural cleavages that cut across the functional and economic divisions in Norwegian society.[77] The issue can also be seen as raising the questions of post-industrial politics, those of the environment, culture, women's rights and democratization.[78] If that is the case, it would seem that the majority of Norwegian voters were not prepared to turn to the EU for answers to those questions. Norway's oil wealth and consequent strong economic situation allowed them to make their decision with some impunity.

Short of a major deterioration in the security situation in Europe, it is unlikely that any Norwegian government will renew the membership application this century. Should the nature of the EU change over the next ten years, with an extension of membership to central and east European states and with a more 'variable geometry' approach to policy, the Norwegian electorate may consider that the costs of membership are worth paying. Meanwhile, a majority of Norwegians seem content to pursue their own economic and political agenda outside the EU.

Bibliography

Aftenposten, 23 September 1972; 6 July 1993; 9 March 1994; 16 April 1994.

Agence Europe (1993), no. 5946, 24 March, p. 7; no. 5947, 25 March, p. 5.; no.5955, 5/6 April; no. 6018, 9 July 1993.

Allen, H. (1979), *Norway and Europe in the 1970s*, Universitetsforlaget, Oslo.

Archer, C. (1971), 'Nordek: shadow or substance?' *Integration*, no. 2, pp.108-16.

Archer, C. (1993), 'Norway Cools to Europe in Election', *The World Today*, vol. 49, no. 12, December, pp. 224-5.

Bjørklund, T. (1982), *Mot strømmen. Kampen mot EF 1961-1972*, Universitetsforlaget, Oslo.

Bjørklund, T. (1994), 'En reprise fra 1972', *Dagbladet*, 30 November 1994, p. 3.

Churchill, R. and Ulfstein, G. (1992), *Marine management in disputed areas: The case of the Barents Sea*, Routledge, London and New York.

Commission of the European Communities (1992a), 'The Challenge of Enlargement: Commission's Opinion on Sweden's Application for Membership', *Bulletin of the European Communities, Supplement 5/92*, Brussels.

Commission of the European Communities (1992b), 'The Challenge of Enlargement: Commission's Opinion on Finland's Application for Membership', *Bulletin of the European Communities, Supplement 6/92*, Brussels.

Commission of the European Communities (1993), 'The Challenge of Enlargement: Commission's Opinion on Norway's Application for Membership', *Bulletin of the European Communities, Supplement 2/93*, Brussels.

Council of the European Communities Commission of the European Communities (1992), *Treaty on European Union*, Luxembourg, 1992.

Dagbladet, 22 September 1972; 27 October 1993.

Dagens Næringsliv, 24 September 1993; 28 September 1993; 19 October 1993; 9 February 1994.

'Declaration from the Oslo Summit Meeting of the EFTA heads of governments in Oslo, 14-15 March 1989'(1989), *EFTA Bulletin*, no. 2, pp. 4-7.

Economist Intelligence Unit (1993a), *Country Report Norway*, EIU, London, 2nd quarter.

Economist Intelligence Unit (1993b), *Country Report Norway*, EIU, London, 3rd quarter.

Economist Intelligence Unit (1993c), *Country Report Norway*, EIU, London, 4th quarter.

Economist Intelligence Unit (1993/4), *Country Profile Norway*, EIU, London.

Economist Intelligence Unit (1994a), *Country Report Norway*, EIU, London, 2nd quarter.

Economist Intelligence Unit (1995a), *Country Report Norway*, EIU, London, 2nd quarter.

Economist Intelligence Unit (1995b), *Country Report Norway*, EIU, London, 3rd quarter.

Economist Intelligence Unit (1995c), *Country Report Norway*, EIU, London, 4th quarter.

Financial Times, 7 July 1993; 23 July 1993; 2 September 1993.

Folkeavstemningen om EF.Norges offisielle statistikk [The advisory referendum on Norway's accession to the EC, Norway's official statistics] (1972), Statistisk sentralbyrå/Central Bureau of Statistics, Oslo, 1972.

Folkebevegelsens melding om Norges forhold til De Europeiske Fellesskap. Motmeldning til Regjeringens Stortingsmelding nr. 50, 1971-72 [People's Movement's report on Norway's connection to the European Community. Counter-report to the government's *Storting* report no. 50, 1971-72] (1972), Folkebevegelsen mot norsk medlemskap i Fellesmarkedet, Oslo, 1972.

Gerhardsen, T.S. et al (1994), *Sosialdemokratisk Alternativ* [Social democratic alternative], Sosialdemokrater mot EU, Oslo.

Gleditsch, N-P. (1972), 'Generaler og fotfolk i utakt: EF-avgjørelsen i de tre skandinaviske land', *Internasjonal Politikk*, 4B, Supplement, pp. 795-804.

Godal, B.T. (1993), 'Innlegg av handelsminister Bjorn Tore Godal', *UD Informasjon*, no.15, 13 April 1993.

Godal, B.T. (1995), 'Utenriksminister Bjorn Tore Godals redegjorelse for stasjonssefsmotet, Oslo, 22.8.95', *UD Informasjon*, no. 27, 6 September 1995.

Harbo, H. (1993), 'Oljedirektivet - kamp om symboler' [The oil directive - fight about symbols], *Aftenposten*, 18 October 1993.

Hellevik, O. and Gleditsch, N-P. (1973), 'The Common Market Decision in Norway: A Clash between Direct and Indirect Democracy', *Scandinavian Political Studies*, no. 8, pp. 227-235.

Holst, J.J.(1992), 'Looking ahead: some personal reflections', *FD-Informasjon*, no. 1, January 1992.

Krogh, A. (1994), 'Fra tap til?' [From defeat to?], *Dagens Naeringsliv*, 27 December, p. 3.

Lipset, S.M. (1981), 'The revolt against modernity', in Per Torsvik (ed), *Mobilization, Center-Periphery Structures and Nation-Building*, Universitetsforlaget, Oslo, pp. 451-500.

Ministry for Foreign Affairs (1994), *Sweden's negotiations on membership of the European Union*, Ministry for Foreign Affairs, Stockholm.

Nordisk Kontakt (1992a), no. 10.

Nordisk Kontakt (1992b), no. 12.

Nordlys (1994), 15 April 1994.

Nytt fra Norge (1993a), *Norinform*, 31 August 1993, p. 9.

Nytt fra Norge (1993b), *Norinform*, 12 October 1993.

Nytt fra Norge (1994), *Norway Now*, no. 6, medio April.

Olsen, J.H.T. (1993), 'Med gode og rimelige krav' [With acceptable and justifiable demands], *Dagbladet*, 17 July 1993.

Regjeringsutvalget for EF-saker (1990) [Government committee for EC questions], *Statusrapport mars 1990: EFTA-EF forhandlingene. Kartlegging og forberedelser*, Ministry of Foreign Affairs Annex 16, Oslo.

Riste, O. (1994), 'Norge - isolasjonismens siste skanse?', *Aftenposten*, 1 December 1994, p. 19.

Rokkan, S. (1970), *Citizens, elections, parties*, Universitetsforlaget, Oslo.

The Royal Ministry of Foreign Affairs (1992), *UD-informasjon*, Oslo, no. 40.

The Royal Ministry of Foreign Affairs (1994), *Norway Daily*, Oslo, no. 6, 10 January 1994; no. 7, 11 January 1994; no. 29, 10 February 1994; no. 184, 23 September 1994; no. 221, 15 November 1994.

The Royal Ministry of Foreign Affairs (1995), *Norway Daily*, Oslo, no. 1, 2 January 1995; no. 5, 6 January 1995; no. 11, 16 January 1995.

Statistics Norway (1995), *Okonomiske analyser*, Statistisk sentralbyra, Oslo.

St.meld (Stortingsmelding) (1986-1987), *Norge, EF og europeisk samarbeid*, Utenriksdepartementet, Oslo, no. 61.

St.meld (Stortingsmelding) (1993-1994), *Om medlemskap i Den europeiske union*, Utenriksdepartementet, Oslo, no. 40.

St.tid (Stortingstidninger) [Parliamentary Debates] (1989-90), 20 November 1989, cols. 565-70; 1 December 1989, cols. 1075-1153.

Thomas, M. (1993), 'The effects of the new EC system', *Euroil*, August 1993, pp. 20-1.

Valen, H. (1973), 'Norway: "No" to EEC', *Scandinavian Political Studies*, no. 8, pp. 215-226.

Valen, H. (1994), 'Norge sa nei for annen gang', *Aftenposten*, 2 December 1994, p. 13.

Notes

1. Research for this chapter was undertaken by the author and Ingrid Sogner, to whom the author is indebted, for a project entitled *Norway and Europe: Security and Political Implications*, and supported by the Economic and Social Research Council's grant no. R000233844. A part version of this article was published in the Journal of Common Market Studies, vol. 33, no. 3, September 1995, pp. 389-410.

2. *Agence Europe*, no. 5946, 24 March 1993, p. 7, and no. 5947, 25 March 1993, p. 5.

3. Commission of the European Communities, 'The Challenge of Enlargement: the Commission's Opinion on Norway's Application for Membership', *Bulletin of the European Communities*, supplement 2/93, 1993.

4. Archer, C., 'Nordek: Shadow or Substance?', *Integration*, no. 2, pp. 108-16.

5. Bjorkland, T., *Mot strommen. Kampen mot EF 1961-1972*, Universitetsforlaget, Oslo, 1982, pp. 108 and 116.

6. *Folkebevegelsens melding om Norges forhold til De Europeiske Fellesskap. Motmelding til Regjeringens Stortingsmelding nr. 50*, People's Movement report on Norway's connection to the European Community (counter-report to the government's Stortong report no. 50, 1971-2), Folkebevegelsen mot norsk medlemskap i Fellesmarkedet, Oslo, 1972.

7. The coalition consisted of the Centre Party, which opposed EC membership, the Christian Peoples Party and the Liberals, both of which were split, and the Conservative Party, which supported membership.

8. Valen, H., 'Norway: "No" to EEC', *Scandinavian Political Studies*, no. 8, pp. 215-26.

9. 'Declaration from the Oslo Summit Meeting of the EFTA Heads of Government, 14-15 March 1989', *EFTA Bulletin*, no. 2, 1989, pp. 4-7.

10. The European Chapter, points 3 and 5, of the government's 'Lysebu Declaration' of October 1989, can be seen in Regjeringsutvalget for EF-saker (1990).

11. Trade Minister Kaci Kullmann Five reported on the EC-EFTA process to the *Storting* (parliament) on 20 November 1989 (St. tid.,1989-90, cols. 565-570) and about possible Norwegian adjustment to the EC's internal market.

12. Economist Intelligence Unit, *Country Report Norway*, London, 4th Quarter, pp. 10-11.

13. Holst, J.J., 'Looking ahead: some personal reflections', *FD-Informasjon*, nr. 1, January 1992.

14. 'Om medlemskap i den Europeiske Union', *Stortingsmelding*, Utenriksdepartementet, Oslo, no. 40, 1993-4.

15. Economist Intelligence Unit, *Country Report Norway*, 3rd Quarter, 1993, p.3.

16. *The Financial Times*, 7 July 1993.

17. Olsen, J.H.T., 'Med gode og rimelige krav' (With acceptable and justifiable demands), *Dagbladet*, 17 July 1993.

18. Olsen, J.H.T., op cit and Godal, B.T., 'Innlegg av handelsminister Bjorn Tore Godal', *UD Informasjon*, no. 15, 13 April 1993.

19. 'Om medlemskap i Den Europeiske Union', *Stortingsmelding*, op cit, pp. 433-4.

20. The Royal Ministry of Foreign Affairs, *Norway Daily*, no. 29, 10 February 1994, p. 1.

21. 'Om medlemskap i den Europeiske Union', *Stortingsmelding*, op cit, p. 225.

22. The Royal Ministry of Foreign Affairs, *Norway Daily*, Oslo, no. 7, 11 January 1994, p. 1.

23. Churchill, R. and Ulfstein, G., *Marine Management in Disputed Areas: The Case of the Barents Sea*, Routledge, London, 1992.

24. Commission of the European Communities, 'The Challenge of Enlargement: Commission's Opinion on Norway's Application for Membership', *Bulletin of the European Communities*, op cit, p. 17.

25. 'Om medlemskap i den Europeiske Union', *Stortingsmelding*, op cit, p. 43; *The Financial Times*, 23 July 1993.

26. *Aftenposten*, 9 March 1994, p. 6 and 16 April 1994; *Nordlys*, 15 April 1994.

27. Nytt fra Norge, *Norway Now*, no. 6, medio April 1994, p. 7.

28. 'Om medlemskap i den Europeiske Union;, *Stortingsmelding*, op cit, pp. 449-50.

29. *Dagbladet*, 22 September 1992; *Aftenposten*, 23 September 1972.

30. Economist Intelligence Unit, *Country Report Norway*, London, 4th Quarter, 1993, p. 10.

31. *Dagens Næringsliv*, 28 September 1993.

32. Economist Intelligence Unit, *Country Report Norway*, London, 4th Quarter 1993, p. 10.

33. Harbo, H., 'Oljedirektivet - kamp om symboler' (The Oil Directive - fight about symbols), *Aftenposten*, 18 October 1993.

34. Nytt fra Norge, *Norinform*, 31 August 1993, p. 9.

35. Economist Intelligence Unit, *Country Report Norway*, London, 4th Quarter 1993, p. 16.

36. 'Om medlemskap i den Europeiske Union', *Stortingsmelding*, op cit, pp. 186-7.

37. Thomas, M., 'The effects of the new EC system', *Euroil*, August 1993, pp. 20-1.

38. *Agence Europe*, no. 5955, 5 April 1993.

39. Economist Intelligence Unit, *Country Report Norway*, London, 2nd Quarter, 1994.

40. Commission of the European Communities, *The Challenge of Enlargement: Commission's Opinion on Norway's Application for Membership*, op cit, p. 16.

41. *Dagens Næringsliv*, 24 September 1993.

42. Economist Intelligence Unit, *Country Report Norway*, London, 2nd Quarter, 1994.

43. Gerhardsen, T.S. et al, *Sosialdemokratisk Alternativ* (Social Democratic Alternative), Sosialdemokrater mot EU, Oslo, 1994.

44. The Royal Ministry of Foreign Affairs, *Norway Daily*, Oslo, no. 6, 10 January 1994, p. 1.

45. Ministry for Foreign Affairs, *Sweden's Negotiations on Membership of the European Union*, Stockholm, 1994, p. 7.

46. Commission of the European Communities, 'The Challenge of Enlargement: Commission's Opinion on Sweden's Application for Membership', *Bulletin of the European Communities*, Supplement no. 5, 1992, p. 27.

47. Commission of the European Communities, 'The Challenge of Enlargement: Commission's Opinion on Finland's Application for Membership', Bulletin of the European Communities, Supplement no. 6, 1992, p. 32.

48. Krogh, A., 'Fra tap til?' (From Defeat too?), *Dagens Næringsliv*, 27 December 1994, p. 3.

49. The Royal Ministry of Foreign Affairs, *Norway Daily*, no. 184, 1994, p. 1.

50. Bjorklund, T., *Mot Strommen: Kampen mot EF 1961-1972*, Universitetsforlaget, Oslo, 1982, pp. 148-54.

51. Economist Intelligence Unit, *Country Report Norway*, London, 4th Quarter, 1993. To join the EU, Sweden had to have membership accepted in two parliamentary sessions with an election in between (see Chapter 5 above). The advisory referendum was held on 13 November 1994, with a general election in September 1994. The hoped-for 'Swedish effect' by the Norwegian 'Yes' campaign - sceptical voters deciding that Norway should follow Finland and Sweden - could perhaps be seen in the opinion polls after that date (The Royal Ministry for Foreign Affairs, 15 November 1994), but it proved to be much smaller than expected.

52. *Nordisk Kontakt*, no. 10 and no. 12; *The Financial Times*, 2 September 1993.

53. Archer, C., 'Norway cools to Europe in Election', *The World Today*, vol. 49, no. 12, pp. 224-5.

54. *Dagbladet*, 27 October 1993.

55. Nytt fra Norge, *Norinform*, 12 October 1993, p. 2.

56. Valen, H., 'Norge sa nei for annen gang', *Aftenposten*, 2 December 1994, p. 13.

57. Valen, H., 'Norway: "No" to EEC', *Scandinavian Political Studies*, no. 8, pp. 215-26.

58. The Royal Ministry of Foreign Affairs, *Norway Daily*, Oslo, no. 11, 1995, p. 2.

59. Bjorklund, T., 'En reprise fra 1972', *Dagbladet*, 30 November 1994, p. 3.

60. *Ibid*.

61. Valen, H., 'Norge sei nei for annen gang', *Aftenposten*, op cit, p. 13.

62. Economist Intelligence Unit, *Country Report Norway*, London, 4th Quarter, 1995, p. 13.

63. *Statistics Norway*, 1995, Table C1.

64. *Ibid*, p. 23.

65. *Ibid*, p. 16.

66. *Ibid*, p. 10.

67. *The Guardian*, 2 November 1995, p. 2.

68. The Royal Ministry of Foreign Affairs, *Norway Daily*, no. 1, 1995, p. 1.

69. The Royal Ministry of Foreign Affairs, *Norway Daily*, no. 5, 1995, p. 1.

70. Economist Intelligence Unit, *Country Report Norway*, London, 2nd Quarter, 1995, pp. 7-8.

71. *Ibid*, p. 8.

72. Economist Intelligence Unit, *Country Report Norway*, London, 3rd Quarter, 1995, p. 9.

73. Economist Intelligence Unit, *Country Report Norway*, London, 3rd Quarter 1995, p. 9.

74. Godal, B.T., 'Utenriksminister Bjorn Tore Godals redegjorelse for Stasjonssefsmotet', *Informasjon*, no. 27, 6 September 1995, p. 5.

75. Economist Intelligence Unit, *Country Report Norway*, London, 4th Quarter, 1995, p. 7.

76. *Ibid*, pp. 17-19.

77. Rokkan, S., *Citizens, Elections, Parties*, Universitetsforlaget, Oslo, 1970, pp. 235-7.

78. Lipset, S.M., 'The Revolt against modernity' in *Mobilization, Centre-Periphery Structures and Nation-building*, edited by Per Torsvik, Universitetsforlaget, Oslo, 1981, p. 470.

8 Conclusion

JOHN REDMOND and ADRIAN TREACHER

The 1995 enlargement and the EU institutions[1]

As with previous enlargements, the three countries acceding in 1995 accepted the *acquis communautaire* - that is, all the existing treaties of the EU (and the related acts) up to, and including, the Treaty of European Union (TEU). The only partial exceptions to this were the existing EU's commitment to review some policy areas, notably environmental standards, and several derogations (but only for up to five years).

The adjustments to the EU institutions, with the exception of the Council of Ministers, were relatively mechanical and were as follows:

- The Commission was increased from 17 to 20 members, thereby giving a Commissioner to each new member;
- The membership of the European Parliament (EP) was increased from 567 to 626, an increase of 59, with 22 from Sweden, 21 from Austria and 16 from Finland. In the first instance, representatives were to be chosen by national parliaments, but direct elections of MEPs were to take place before the end of 1996;
- The number of judges in the European Court of Justice was increased from 13 to 15; the (thirteenth) 'extra' judge (to ensure an uneven number) was dropped and the three new members each have a judge. In addition, the number of advocates-general was increased from six to nine (with the three new member states participating in a system of alphabetical rotation);
- The Court of Auditors and the Court of First Instance were both enlarged from 12 to 15 members, thereby providing each of the three new members with their own appointee;
- The Economic and Social Committee and the Committee of the Regions were each expanded from 189 to 222 members (an increase of 33), with 12 new members each from Austria and Sweden and 9 from Finland.

All this proved to be relatively straightforward. However, this was not the case with the changes to the Council.

The Council was subject to two significant adjustments. The first of these was relatively uncontroversial. It involved abandoning the traditional, alphabetical system of rotation of its presidency and replacing it with a new system which sought to do two things: first, to make sure that at least one of the five largest EU member states was always part of the Council troika and, second, to avoid the three new members holding the presidency consecutively.[2]

The second change was rather controversial and involved the voting rights of member states. In the post-enlargement system, Austria and Sweden were given four votes each and Finland three. This raised the total number of votes in the Council from 76 to 87, the votes required for a qualified majority from 54 to 62 (to be normally cast by ten rather than eight countries) and, implicitly, the 'blocking minority' from 23 to 27 votes. This was opposed by the Spanish, because it undermined the blocking power of the Mediterranean group, and by the British on more general grounds. Eventually, in March 1994, the Ionnina Compromise was reached whereby it was agreed that if three countries with 23-25 votes opposed a decision, then the Council would 'do all in its power to reach, within a reasonable time ... a satisfactory solution that could be adopted by at least sixty five votes'.[3] This is clearly ill-defined and awaits clarification (or replacement) at the 1996 intergovernmental conference (IGC).

Beyond 1995: future enlargements of the European Union

Clearly, the institutional changes in 1995 represented mainly numerical adjustments rather than radical reform. This will not be the case for future enlargements as the Rome Treaty mechanisms have now reached their limit; subsequent enlargements will require major restructuring. Thus, the 1995 accessions are the last ones to which the 'traditional' classical enlargement method[4] will have been applied. The classical method involves only minimal change for the existing EU membership; new members are simply tacked on to the current EU structure with minor adjustments to institutions and policies. Post-1995 enlargements will be 'adaptive' - they will create the need for a transformation of the EU's structures and policies.

The formal debate over the reform of the institutional system began in the Reflection Group, established in July 1995 to prepare for the 1996 IGC. A number of issues were raised in the Group's first report:[5]

- For the Commission, a crucial issue is a size - particularly whether its growth should be restrained - which might imply one Commissioner for each country (small and large) and/or smaller countries having to 'share' a Commissioner. In addition, the Commission's monopoly of legislative initiative is also under scrutiny;
- The control of size is also important to the EP for which an upper limit of 700 has been suggested. This would imply less MEPs for the existing membership;
- In the Council, the key issues relate to the voting system - the extension of majority voting, the size of the qualified majority (and the blocking minority), and the possible reform of the system to prevent situations whereby a qualified majority might be mustered by a group of small countries representing less than half the EU's population. This latter point is particularly difficult to resolve. Three possibilities have been put forward: a new system of weighting, changing the threshold for qualified majorities or the introduction of a double majority (votes and population); all of these would be controversial.

The issue of the continuance of over-representation of smaller countries in EU institutions is clearly of particular importance to the three members who joined in 1995.

Subsequent enlargement of the EU will also require a radical transformation of policies. To some extent, this has already begun with agriculture but the accession of the CEECs will require much more extensive reform of the Common Agricultural Policy (CAP) if expenditure is to remain within acceptable limits. Similarly, the implications for unmodified structural funds would be immense and so reform is also needed there. Since the CAP and the Structural Funds together account for 80 per cent of the EU's expenditure, much of the change will work through the budget. As net contributors in the further enlarged EU, with a tradition of heavily supported agricultural sectors, Austria, Finland and Sweden will clearly take a great interest in these reforms. Another area of serious concern to the three new members, on which any accession of the CEECs will particularly impact, is environmental policy. Finally, the accession of the relatively economically weak CEECs and Mediterranean applicants will not be helpful for the achievement of economic and monetary union

(EMU). All of them will struggle with the economic convergence criteria in the immediate future and some will continue to do so for a very long time.

The conflict between enlargement and EMU highlights another fundamental concern: the widening versus deepening debate. This has been ongoing since before the EU's first enlargement and the potentially conflictual relationship between the two was very much recognised in the period immediately before the 1995 enlargement. Initially, in the mid-1980s, when the only source of applications for membership appeared to be EFTA, the EU sought to ward off widening by offering EFTA the EEA. After the Mediterranean applications and the dramatic events in eastern Europe, when it became clear that countries from all corners of Europe were likely to pursue EU accession, the EU produced and progressively extended the list of internal business that had to be completed before enlargement could be considered;[6] this amounted to an attempt to get the deepening into place before widening commenced, thereby avoiding any conflict between the two, because new members would have to accept the recently agreed deepening as part of the *acquis communautaire*.

In fact, the 1995 enlargement introduces obvious elements of potential conflict. All three new members are only recent converts to the pursuit of EU-style European integration and there are strong suspicions that this conversion is pragmatic rather than genuine. Consequently, it is uncertain to what extent they will wish to advance down many of the paths that have been mapped out by the EU's Franco-German core. The dubious reasons (from a federalist perspective) that led these countries to change their minds and join (crystallised in the 'integration dilemma') have been described in the introduction. There inevitably is apprehension about the compatibility of the 1995 widening with the deepening agenda laid out in the TEU. For example, despite the relative ease with which the CFSP (common foreign and security policy) was covered during the accession negotiations, the neutrality of the three new members must raise doubts about their support for the further development of this policy; meanwhile, on the economic front, Finland and Sweden have not joined the ERM and, more generally, the EU may now harbour a 'dissident' Anglo-Nordic group.

Enlargement beyond fifteen will highlight other more obvious frictions between widening and deepening. These include the diversion of effort and the distraction that widening causes and the strain on the institutions and individual policies of the EU.[7] However, the biggest conflict may increasingly arise from the sheer size and diversity of the EU's membership. The most insidious and influential aspect of the constraint on deepening imposed by widening remains the acceptance as full members of more and more countries not committed to the vision of European integration espoused by the EU's founding fathers.

Beyond 1995: the positions of Austria, Finland and Sweden[8]

Countries acceding to the EU before 1995 have been characterised as following the classical model, which basically involves accepting the *acquis communautaire*. Post-1995 enlargements will be adaptive: new members cannot be so certain of what EU membership will actually mean because the very act of their accession will change the Union (quite possibly in such a way that they may actually not become members of the EU they thought they were going to, or indeed wanted to, join). Although 1995 was characterised above as the last of the classical enlargements, the three countries joining in 1995 actually find themselves somewhere inbetween the classical and adaptive modes of accession. They have accepted the *acquis communautaire* but, exceptionally, can play a role in determining much of it, in effect, retrospectively. The 1995 enlargement is thus unique. The countries which acceded in 1995 are being given preferential treatment amongst the 'outsiders' who were driven to pursue EU membership from the late 1980s. They have been given a seat at the table where critical decisions about the future development of the EU will be taken which will not be offered to the CEEC and Mediterranean applicants; indeed it is a privileged position which Norway (and Switzerland) may one day regret rejecting.

In general, there is much agreement between the three new members over the preferred future direction of the EU. They might all be considered 'Euro-sceptical' to a degree, although Austria does have leanings towards the 'Franco-German/founding fathers' position, and Sweden is perhaps more 'extreme' than Finland in its 'Euro-scepticism'. Sweden and Finland also have specific 'Nordic' views, many (but not all) of which Austria supports. The general policy stances of the three new members will be especially important and they can be expected to be along the following lines:

- The position of the smaller states has to be safeguarded; for example, whilst a down-sized Commission is not opposed, the principle of one Commissioner per member state is strongly upheld. Similarly, it is recognised that a smaller EP may be necessary but that this should not be achieved at the expense of the representation of the smaller states. Not surprisingly, the proposal that the weighting of votes in the Council should, to some extent, reflect population size attracts little support. The 1995 enlargement will thus significantly strengthen the hand of the Benelux countries which have traditionally defended the role of smaller members;

- There is general support for the use of the principle of subsidiarity, although for a mixture of motives. For the Austrians, it is perhaps mostly a matter of principle, but the Scandinavians are more pragmatic. While the Finns see it as a useful device but one which is essentially political rather than legal, and which should be applied selectively so as not to impede the transfer of appropriate policy activities (such as environmental protection) to the European level. The Swedish view is that a well balanced application of the principle of subsidiarity offers a desirable alternative to the development of a federal EU;

- A single-tier (but not necessarily single-speed) EU is the favoured model of the three new members, although support is qualified in the Swedish case. Austria regards 'differentiated' integration as very much the exception with 'phased' integration the norm, except where this would give an unfair competitive advantage to the slower countries; the Austrians have in mind the British opt-out from the EU's social policy as a prime example of unfair advantage. Finland is perhaps even more enthusiastic, dismissing 'memberships of different classes' and seeing different speeds as exceptional. Swedish views tend to go in the other direction: although there is a presumption in favour of a single-tier, single-speed EU on the grounds that deviation from this may undermine the single market, differentiated integration is not discarded as it offers a degree of flexibility which it is thought may be desirable; this position may well reflect Swedish distaste for a federal EU;

- On the form that future European integration should take, Austria is inclined to be the most indulgent towards any drift towards a more federal Europe and is, for example, cautious about, but willing to discuss, an increase in the use of majority voting in the Council. On the other hand, Sweden is quite clear that it does not wish the EU to develop along federal lines and the Finns favour the continuation of the EU as 'an association of independent states'. The two Nordics are also generally opposed to any shift away from intergovernmentalism (as the form of cooperation) in the CFSP and JHA (justice and home affairs) pillars of the EU.

The three new members - and Sweden and Finland, in particular - thus appear to have potentially inconsistent views. A single-tier, and ideally single-speed, EU is preferred, but this preference co-exists with a strong propensity towards intergovernmentalism and against federalism, which conflicts with the views of several, older, key members of the EU.

More specifically, the 1995 cohort is very keen to push forward EU development in a number of areas. There is much concern to strengthen the EU's democratic legitimacy, to increase transparency, openness and the provision of information, and to develop the concept of citizenship in an EU context. This is all partly connected to the need to maintain popular support for the EU which has declined in all three new members, so much so that referenda at the end of the first year of membership would have produced 'no' votes in Austria and Sweden.[9] Strongly favoured policy areas include the environment, social policy and the 'fight against unemployment'; indeed, the Finns are inclined to support more majority voting (in the Council) in order to accelerate environmental and social policies. There is a common desire to see the JHA pillar function more effectively and equally to develop the CFSP, but to limit its scope to the so-called Petersberg tasks agreed for the Western European Union (conflict management, peacekeeping operations and humanitarian aid); there is wariness about the development of a common defence policy. However, there are differences - Austria is willing to allow a gradual integration of the CFSP into the Community framework while Sweden and Finland prefer continued intergovernmental cooperation in this area. Similarly, on economic and monetary union, whereas Austria is keen to participate in the third phase from the beginning, Sweden and Finland, like Britain, reserve the right for their parliaments to decide on this at the appropriate time.

Finally, the 1995 enlargement enhances the 'Nordic dimension' within the EU, as Denmark is now joined by Sweden and Finland. Elements of this - notably concern with the environment - are strongly supported by Austria but there are others: notably, concepts of gender, equality and social justice, and 'northern' natural conditions and low population density which lead to particular perspectives on EU agricultural, transport and regional/structural policies. The Nordics also wish to champion the cases for EU membership of the Baltic states and are seeking to bracket their applications with those of the CEECs, Cyprus and Malta; in addition, of course, the EU now has a land border with Russia. However, perhaps the most critical aspect of the Nordic dimension is their predilection for intergovernmentalism, which originally led to their participation in EFTA rather than the EU (then EEC).

Beyond the development of a Nordic bloc there is a perception, particularly amongst the EU's southern member states, that the 1995 enlargement will encourage a more northern bias inside the Union. There already exists, within the EU, marked differences in policy preferences and priorities between north and south and the accession of three 'northern' states may prove to be detrimental to the preferences of the EU's Mediterranean members. Furthermore, this latest enlargement, particularly the inclusion of Austria, is also likely to accentuate traditional concerns about German dominance of the EU, fuelled in recent years by German reunification. Thus, in addition to the obvious addition of a distinct Nordic dimension within the EU, the potential strengthening of the northern/German focus should not be underestimated.

The 1995 enlargement of the EU is thus likely to have a significant effect on the future course of the Union. Austria, Sweden and Finland are rich, developed and articulate countries which did not seek EU membership from a position of political and/or economic weakness. They will add a new dimension to the EU by championing the environment, social policy, transparency and citizenship and will strengthen the position of the smaller member states. They will question federalism and will, on balance, make the EU more intergovernmental in outlook, at least in the short run. Indeed, despite their preference to the contrary, their accessions may hasten the emergence of a multi-tier Europe.

Beyond 1995: variable geometry?

The likelihood of a variable geometry EU follows on from the contention that an Anglo-Nordic 'dissident' bloc has emerged after the 1995 enlargement. The tensions will increase - and, indeed, accelerate further - if the CEECs join, between those who favour a more deeply integrated EU and those who prefer a much looser intergovernmental arrangement. It will become increasingly difficult for the two groups to co-exist within the present single-speed, single-tier EU. If the laggards are unprepared to pursue the Maastricht agenda seriously, then those member states wishing to deepen more extensively may feel compelled to establish an inner circle for fast-track integration. This line of thinking was signalled even before the 1995 accessions: in 1994, a German CDU/CSU paper[10] proposed a hard core of five countries (the EU's original six members minus Italy) which must 'participate as a matter of course in all policy fields', give 'the Union a strong centre to counteract the centrifugal forces generated by constant enlargement', and which 'must be open to every member state willing and able to meet its requirements'.[11] This would appear to advocate that deepening must continue and, if it is threatened by lack of agreement, then interested countries should proceed unilaterally even at the cost of allowing a multi-speed EU to emerge.[12]

The precise form this would take is uncertain and, indeed, the expression 'variable geometry' is frequently used very loosely. In fact there are a number of possibilities:

- A single-speed EU is where every member state participates fully in every stage in every policy. The EU has actually not been single-speed since its first enlargement in 1973. This is partly because there has nearly always since been one or more new members in a transition stage and, therefore with a variety of temporary derogations. However, more fundamentally, since 1972 the various exchange rate mechanisms - the 'snake' in the 1970s and the ERM of the European Monetary System thereafter - have always involved partial membership with non-participants expected to 'catch up' in due course.
- A single-tier EU is where every member state is pursuing the same group of policies but not necessarily at the same speed. Thus, whilst a single-tier EU may also be single-speed, it is quite possible to have a single-tier, multi-speed EU[13] and indeed, this is precisely what occurred from 1973 until 1992 when the British and Danish opt-outs from the TEU made the EU *de facto* multi-tier or, perhaps better, à la carte (see below).
- A multi-speed EU is where every member is included in every policy in principal[14] but, in practice, each member is moving at a different speed. As indicated above, the EU has arguably become this already. Provided a unity of purpose in the shape of a common end objective survives, and the majority of policies remain single-speed, then a multi-speed arrangement is relatively uncontroversial. It is simply a politically expedient device for allowing those who can and wish to go further to do so whilst giving the laggards time to catch up.
- A multi-tier EU (or EU of concentric circles) is where there is no common end goal. It is not a question of different speeds but different destinations. The EU is comprised of an inner tier implementing all policies, a second tier consisting of a group of countries which have opted out of an (identical) subset of EU policies, a third tier with an opt out from a larger subset of policies, and so on. (The tiers could all be single or multi-speed or some could be single and some multi-speed.)

- A Europe à la carte or 'pick-and-choose Europe', to use the Commission's rather derogatory phrase,[15] is where each member state chooses to opt into or out of each policy; there will probably (but, in principal, not necessarily) be a hard core of countries which participate in all or at least a group of central policies. The order of a multi-tier arrangement is lost as each member is effectively a tier on its own.

It is these last two arrangements that are controversial because they would establish a very different EU to the one that currently exists. The critical issue is not whether the EU becomes multi-speed - to some extent, it already is - but whether it becomes multi-tier. The key is whether non-participation stems from technical - often economic - reasons (necessity) or political reasons (choice).

The implication of this debate is that the concept of 'membership' ceases to be fixed but becomes variable. The 1995 cohort of new members is uniquely placed to take advantage of this situation. The countries joining later will have to accept membership of the EU as defined (and offered) by the existing membership. However, Austria, Finland and Sweden can actually help shape what EU membership will mean for them. Whilst they had to accept the *acquis communautaire*, a key part of this - the Maastricht agenda - was effectively only loosely defined, and they will actually have a role in determining the detail at the 1996 IGC. The 1995 enlargement was a key event in the history of the EU; it may also eventually be seen as marking a critical turning point in the development of the Union.

Notes

1.   This section draws heavily on D. Phinnemore, 'The 1995 enlargement and the EU's Treaties', *European Access*, no. 1, February 1995, pp. 8-10.

2.   Thus the order of presidencies from 1995 to 2003 is as follows: France, Spain (1995); Italy, Ireland (1996); Netherlands, Luxembourg (1997); UK, Austria (1998); Germany, Finland (1999); Portugal, France (2000); Sweden, Belgium (2001); Spain, Denmark (2002); Greece (2003). In 1998, Netherlands is effectively treated as a 'large' country.

3.   *Official Journal of the European Union*, no. C105, 13 April 1994, p. 1.

4.   Preston, C. (1995), 'Obstacles to EU Enlargement: The Classical Community Methods and the Prospects for a Wider Europe', *Journal of Common Market Studies*, vol. 33, no. 3, September.

5.   *Progress Report from the Chairman of the Reflection Group on the 1996 Intergovernmental Conference*, September 1995, reproduced by Agence Europe, *Europe Documents*, no. 1951/2, 27 September 1995. For a Commission view, see European Commission (1996), *Intergovernmental conference 1996: Commission Opinion: Reinforcing political union and preparing for enlargement* (Luxembourg), pp. 19-22.

6.   Initially, the Commission stated that the 1992 single market programme had to be completed before any enlargement of the EU could be contemplated; then it added the agreement of the 'Delors II' budget package (the post-1992 financial perspective) and then the ratification of the (Maastricht) Treaty of European Union (although, in fact, negotiations for the 1995 enlargement began before this was fully resolved).

7.   For a fuller discussion, see Redmond, J. (1995), 'Widening versus Deepening or Widening and Deepening? Enlarging the European Union in the 1990s' in *Europe at the Crossroads*, edited by A. Cox and P. Furlong (Boston: Earlsgate Press).

8.   Much of the material on which this section is based is drawn from EU sites on the internet, particularly: http//:www.cec.lu/en/agenda/igc-home/index.html

9.   Yrjö Venna (1995), 'EU-Finland: first-year impressions', *EIPASCOPE*, no. 3, p. 11.

10.   'Reflections on European Policy', reproduced in K. Lamers, *A German Agenda for European Union*, Federal Trust, London, 1994.

11.   *Ibid*, p. 17.

12.   An obvious model would be the Schengen Agreement.

13.   Similarly, it is possible to have a multi-tier, single speed EU in the sense of having a number of tiers of membership, pursuing different subsets of EU policies, but with all the members within each tier implementing their group of policies at the same speed.

14.   Or, alternatively, in a multi-tier arrangement, where every member in each tier is included in every policy adhered to by that tier.

15.   Commission (1996), op cit, p. 21.

Index